Moon of the soul accompany me now,
Shine on the colloseums of my sense,
Be in the tabernacles of my brow.
My dark will make, reflecting from your stones,
The single beam of all my life intense.

"Vita Nuova"   STANLEY KUNITZ

PLATE 1

PHILIP GUSTON'S

Poem-Pictures

Addison Gallery of American Art

Phillips Academy

Andover, Massachusetts 01810

508.749.4015

The Addison Gallery is a Department of Phillips Academy.

This catalogue accompanies the exhibition *Philip Guston's Poem-Pictures* organized by the Addison Gallery of American Art in association with The American Federation of Arts. The exhibition and catalogue are funded by Refco Group Ltd., the National Endowment for the Arts, a Federal agency, Mr. and Mrs. Werner H. Kramarsky, and Jacob and Ruth Kainen.

Library of Congress Catalog Card Number: 94–72273

ISBN 1–879886–38–3

Photography by

Greg Heins, Boston, MA: pls. 1–2, 6–8, 11–24, 29, 37–41, fig. 1

Robert Mates: pls. 4, 32–36

Spectrum Color Labs, Boston, MA: pls. 3, 31, 39

Ben E. Watkins Photography: pls. 9, 26–28

Design by Sally Abugov

Printed by LaVigne Press

cover: Clark Coolidge and Phillip Guston, *...The Painter Can't Sleep for Sight Won't Move,* Collection of Clark Coolidge

The act of painting: Drawing the boundaries of a fire.

CLARK COOLIDGE

P.g.

PLATE 3

Philip Guston's

Poem-Pictures

Debra Bricker Balken

with contributions by

Bill Berkson

Clark Coolidge

William Corbett

Stanley Kunitz

Addison Gallery of American Art

Phillips Academy, Andover, Massachusetts

University of Washington Press

Seattle and London

Lenders to the Exhibition

Gallery Paule Anglim

Philip Anglim

Bill Berkson

Jay Boggis

Clark Coolidge

William Corbett

Lisa and Stuart Ginsberg

Musa Mayer, Executor of the Estate of Musa Guston

Stanley Kunitz

Edward F. Miller

Michael Palmer

Private Collection, New York

Paul Sack

Ben E. and Judith Watkins

Douglas Watson

Gallery Staff

Alison Cleveland, Administrative Assistant

Brian Coleman, Assistant for Collection Care

Susan C. Faxon, Associate Director and Curator of Paintings, Prints, and Drawings

Denise J.H. Johnson, Registrar

Allison N. Kemmerer, Assistant Curator

Leslie Maloney, Preparator

Juliann D. McDonough, Curatorial Assistant

David Olivares, Security Officer

Jock Reynolds, Director

Hector Rivera, Custodian

Carmel Rodriguez-Walter, Front Desk Attendant

John Sirois, Assistant Preparator

Duncan F. Will, Director of Museum Resources and Public Information

Contents

ALONE WITH THE MOON

What about the small game
and the dew falling?

The dry leaves of autumn
magnify the hop
of the lightest bird.

Why don't you lie down
to pass the time?
Why not sleep – and never meet?

Let the witnesses
be distant mountains.

Should I get back to the city?
To be with the guilty?
Or stay with the tree,
unconscious of me?

musa.

PLATE 4

10

Introduction

This exhibition began with a visit. Knowing of the Addison Gallery's ongoing interest in presenting the work of major figures in American art, Debra Bricker Balken came to see me one day and proposed that the Gallery host a showing of the drawings Philip Guston had created in collaboration with American writers. Much of this work is still little known today, yet it offers fascinating insights into the way Guston thought about life and art in the largest sense and reveals a particularly rich vein of creative collaboration—one of many that were mined in our country's cultural community during the 1960s and 70s.

In the spirit of Guston's original collaborative and interdisciplinary forays, Ms. Balken's project has been embraced here on the campus of Phillips Academy as a special opportunity for intellectual exchange. The Addison Gallery is presenting this exhibition in conjunction with poetry readings and education programs supported by the Oliver Wendell Holmes Library and the Academy's English and Art Departments.

Cooperating further with Kim Sichel and Mary McInnes, our colleagues at Boston University's Art Gallery and Art History Department, we have timed the presentation of Ms. Balken's exhibition to coincide with an excellent showing of Guston's late paintings at the Boston University Art Gallery. The works being shown there were all created during Guston's final working years, a time during which he taught at Boston University and exerted a strong influence on many young students and artists.

The national tour of this exhibition is being facilitated by The American Federation of Arts, which has generously collaborated with the Addison in co-producing Ms. Balken's project. Our colleagues at the AFA, Serena Rattazzi, Robert Workman, Thomas Padon, Evie Klein, Sarah Higby, Gabriela Mizes, and Jillian Slonim, have been a pleasure to work with and considerate in every regard.

There are many other people to thank for bringing this exhibition and publication to fruition. Foremost among them is Musa Guston Mayer, who has from the start been invaluable to this project. She enthusiastically provided reminiscences of her father and mother, loans of artwork and manuscripts, constant good humor, warm hospitality, and unwavering support of Ms. Balken's enterprise. Likewise the poets, Bill Berkson, Clark Coolidge, William Corbett, and Stanley Kunitz, deserve particular acknowledgement and gratitude. Their warm and emotional memories of Guston helped shape Ms. Balken's understanding of him as an artist and a man, and their contributions to the editing of Musa McKim's new poetry anthology *Alone With The Moon* (recently published by Figures Press) are also deeply appreciated. And to Geoffrey Young, the poet and publisher of Figures Press, an old friend of mine and Ms. Balken's, we offer heartfelt thanks for the magical and selfless ways he keeps bringing the lives and work of creative people together. Young, after all, first introduced Ms. Balken to the Guston-Coolidge *Poem-Pictures* and was a champion of Ms. Balken's work when this exhibition was first proposed to the Addison. Young also tipped off me and my wife, Suzanne Hellmuth, to Coolidge's writing in the 1970s and later invited us to design a cover for one of this writer's fine volumes of poems.

David McKee of the David McKee Gallery was a major source of help in locating material for the show. His recollections of Guston's conversations about writers also added valuably to Ms. Balken's interpretations as this project evolved. He and all the lenders to the exhibition have been very kind in sharing their Guston drawings with the public for this show and its tour. We thank them all.

Other colleagues in our field were also a great help to Ms. Balken. Robert Storr and Raphael Rubinstein kindly shared their ideas and interpretations of Guston's interactions with writers, while Richard Fyffe of the Homer Babbidge Library, University of Connecticut/Storrs, which holds the Bill Berkson papers, also thoughtfully assisted Ms. Balken with her research; as did Ms. Balken's research assistant Laura Baptiste who worked on the early phases of inquiry for this show.

The financial support of this exhibition and its publication was generously provided by Refco Group, Ltd. (with special thanks to Frances and Thomas Dittmer), The American Federation of Arts, the National Endowment for the Arts, Mr. and Mrs. Werner H. Kramarsky, Jacob and Ruth Kainen, and the Addison Gallery-Mark Rudkin (PA '47) Publication Fund.

As always, members of the Addison's staff deserve kind thanks for the tireless work they've performed in bringing this project to life. Denise Johnson, our registrar, kindly gathered all the loans for the show, while Alison Cleveland, my assistant, transcribed and helped edit the text for this publication. Susan Faxon, our Associate Director and Curator, along with Allison Kemmerer, Assistant Curator, ably proofed the catalogue's text, while preparators, Leslie Maloney, Brian Coleman, and John Sirois beautifully matted, framed, and installed the exhibition. Juli McDonough, our Curatorial Assistant, contributed her good work to all the labeling of the show, while David Olivares, our Head of Security, and Carmel Rodriguez-Walter warmly greeted our public visitors, students, and teachers. Hector Rivera maintained the gallery in sparkling cleanliness, and Duncan Will, our Director of Public Information and Museum Resources, as always spread the word of this project in many quarters and helped it garner the critical attention it deserves.

There are still other colleagues to thank here on Andover's campus for their interested participation in the Guston project. Sally Abugov worked hard to design another beautiful catalogue for the Addison, working closely with Ms. Balken at every turn. Susan Noble director of the Oliver Wendell Holmes Library, David Cobb chairman of the English department, and Stephen Wicks chairman of the Art department have kindly helped us arrange a host of interesting readings and class visits, and each deserves our gratitude.

Finally, we wish to again thank Debra Bricker Balken for the persistence and clarity of her vision in developing *Philip Guston's Poem-Pictures* for our museum. As a guest working among us, she has been a wonderful colleague, always enthusiastic and ever professional in attending to every detail of her work. Presenting Ms. Balken's, the poets', and Philip Guston's work is a great privilege and honor for the Addison Gallery of American Art.

Jock Reynolds
Director

PLATE 5

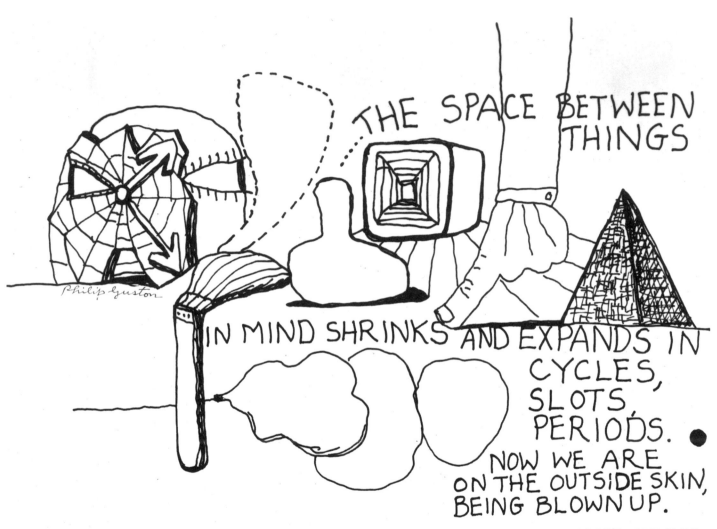

THE SPACE BETWEEN THINGS

Philip Guston

IN MIND SHRINKS AND EXPANDS IN CYCLES, SLOTS PERIODS. ●
NOW WE ARE ON THE OUTSIDE SKIN, BEING BLOWN UP.

CLARK COOLIDGE

PLATE 6

Philip Guston's Poem-Pictures

In my beginning is my end. In succession
Houses rise and fall, crumble, are extended,
Are removed, destroyed, restored, or in their place
Is an open field, or a factory, or a by-pass.
Old stone to new building, old timber to new fires,
Old fires to ashes, and ashes to the earth
Which is already flesh, fur and faeces,
Bone of man and beast, cornstalk and leaf.

T.S. Eliot, *The Four Quartets*

In the ruin history has physically merged into the setting.
And in this guise history does not assume the form of an
eternal life so much as that of irresistible decay. Allegory
thereby declares itself to be beyond beauty. Allegories are,
in the realm of thoughts, what ruins are in the realm of things.

Walter Benjamin, *The Origin of German Tragic Drama*

INTIMATE AND STRANGE SITUATIONS

While Philip Guston had always placed a premium on his associations with poets and writers, during the last decade or so of his life, many of his literary relationships became especially meaningful. For starters, Guston identified with the "oblique things"[1] or unrestrained descriptions that a poet or writer would bring to his work. "They see without the art world lingo," he said, "Sharply. Freshly. Sometimes they're funny, or their reaction funny, and I enjoy that. I don't like writing that's snarled up. It's a cover-up."[2] But his aversion to jargon or "lingo," as he put it, and the frequent incantation of theory in some art-writing ran deeper than aesthetic preference and difference. Somewhere around 1967–68 (the moment is imprecise), Guston effected a stunning transformation of the visual language of his work. He vacated his once graceful and luminous (often referred to as lyrical) abstractions of the late 1940s through mid 1960s in favor of imagery made up of a quirky, incongruous mix of heads, figures of the Ku Klux Klan, and objects such as books, light bulbs, shoes, clocks, and bottles among other pedestrian things.[3]

The critical reception to this new body of work when it was first shown at the Marlborough Gallery, New York City in 1970 could not have been more condemning: the New York School of painters with whom Guston had long been identified and whose work by this point had become thoroughly conventionalized, settled into repetition and complacency, wanted no further affiliation and contact with Guston, with the exception of Willem de Kooning and James Brooks. The press also responded with overwhelming incredulity and disdain, stating sometimes quite directly that a latent lunacy generated these images. In a now legendary review of the exhibition in *The New York Times*, Hilton Kramer made Guston out to be a "mandarin artist pretending to be a stumblebum."[4]

The art world fallout from Guston's programmatic shift resulted in his permanent retreat from New York City to the solitude of rural Woodstock. The company of writers became his primary social and intellectual outlet. As Clark Coolidge, a poet who became a friend of Guston's around 1970, explained, "Getting to know poets and writers was a part of [his] … withdrawal from the New York painter's scene."[5] These new alliances also had a tangible impact on Guston's late work. The texts of many writers were frequently incorporated as integral elements in his work, a feature that adds to its ambiguity and layers of content.

In a letter dated December 28, 1975, to Bill Berkson, a poet, friend, and advocate of Guston's work since the early 1960s, the artist wrote:

> In November, I did Dozens and Dozens of *Poem-Pictures*—Clark, Musa,
> and Corbett poems. … It is a strange form for me—excites me in that it
> does make a *new* thing—a new image—words and images feeding off
> each other in unpredictable ways. Naturally, there is no "illustration" of
> text, yet I am fascinated by how text *and* image bounce into and off
> each other. Of course this happened strongly with Enigma Variations
> text and the drawings—but I think, hope, you'll agree that when it is all
> on one page, a more intimate & STRANGE situation is created—I wish
> you could see what I did with Clark's texts.[6]

Guston's *Poem-Pictures*, as he calls them, comprise a remarkable body of work. The enthusiasm he conveys in his letter to Berkson underscores the significance Guston attached to these pictures, as well as the impact that poetry (and other prose writing) exerted on his late work. These drawings—only three paintings exist which conjoin text and image—stand out within Guston's career through their deft fitting of forms with words as well as within the larger, overall scheme of the history of interactions between artists and writers in the twentieth century.

PLATE 7

That Guston alludes to *Enigma Variations*, a collection of poetry by Bill Berkson with drawings by the artist, in the aforementioned letter is telling. The context of the reference suggests the project was transitional to Guston, a frame for subsequent elaboration on some of the dialectical relationships presented by the duality of image and text. While Guston had created drawings for a number of covers of publications of poetry and prose between 1969 and 1974—works such as *Ing* (a poem by Coolidge), *The World* (pl. 3) and *Big Sky 4* (both anthologies of poetry), *Incidents in the Day World* (a collection of poems by Alice Notley) (pl. 39) and *The Spade in the Sensorium* (a novel by David Anderson)[7]—*Enigma Variations*, 1975 (pl. 11), was Guston's first venture in pairing his drawing with poetry, to establish a connection between language and picture.

The project consisted of a book of some fifteen images juxtaposed with poems. A few of these drawings were pre-existent, now recycled and woven into a new format. As *Enigma Variations* drew on a chronological mix of Berkson's work, Guston felt that the occasional use of earlier, abstract material made for a more direct correspondence between picture and poem, form and content. In a letter to William Corbett, a Boston-based poet, Guston defended the inclusion of his earlier work in the volume: "Since Bill's poems are somewhat retrospective, I selected some drawings of mine which were also. I felt they fit quite well."[8] Yet the book also benefitted from Guston's recent preoccupations. A number of idiosyncratic depictions of shoes, hands, and heads appear along with the abstractions. In fact, he looked upon the manuscript of *Enigma Variations* as an agency, a means to trigger linkages and memories of figures, places, and objects long embedded in the recesses of his psyche. He wrote to Berkson that he would "want to read *Enigma Variations* with lots of Drawing Paper around,"[9] a statement that speaks of a metaphoric dialogue and symbiosis. It also suggests that many of these juxtapositions were not quite so random.

A few precedents exist within the history of Guston's own work for the kind of text/image combinations that run through *Enigma Variations*. Guston had illustrated *The Gift of the Magi* by O. Henry in 1946.[10] A commission rather than pure exchange between artist and writer, the four drawings produced

figure 1. Bill Berkson and Phillip Guston, *Matter*, 1969.

by Guston are more ancillary than equivalents, tied as they are to the narrative. While Guston's own work during this period was poised at a critical juncture, about to veer away from figuration to painting and drawing with few or no external references (a development that interestingly presages the stylistic reversal in Guston's work around 1967–68), the illustrations for the O. Henry allegory are more fixtures or adornments, endowed as they are with all the specificity and facts required to explicate the story. A decade later, with Guston at the height of his involvement in abstraction, with his elimination of the object from painting and evocation of elusive elements such as air, matter, and various states of feeling (especially brooding), Robert Creeley transposed into writing something of the ambiguity of the artist's new work:

> I think—in that denseness of anxieties, and sorrows, like a nightmare
> world, of forms which are all exact and there, yet not the forms? What are
> the forms, one says. It is not possible that one should not arrive at them.[11]

These lines from a poem (Creeley refers to the piece as "a note") were written as a response, a kind of ode, which appeared in a journal next to a suite of reproductions of Guston's abstractions. Unlike the illustrations for *The Gift of the Magi* which take their cues from the story, the Creeley/Guston juxtaposition operates more on the level of creative exchange or reciprocity. Admittedly, Creeley's "note" feeds from Guston's work, but it also abides by its own internal logic, has a separate identity as a poem, and could stand on its own without any visual accompaniment. The joining of poem and painting mutually enhance each other. Certain analogies exist in the play on contradiction in both works.

In a similar arrangement Guston's work also appeared alongside a poem by Musa McKim (his wife) in a project on poets and painters orchestrated for *Art in America* in 1965.[12] The results are strikingly different, however. The combination of text and image here elicited more a sense of rupture and discontinuity rather than cohesion. The abstract style of Guston's drawing was basically at odds with the more literal descriptions in McKim's work. A state of tension rather than harmony is suggested by the pairing.

Whatever the outcome, a number of intriguing issues are presented by this juxtaposition. Like the Creeley/Guston union, the duality of text and image makes for a situation that is open-ended and indeterminate, and that ultimately allows for the greater possibility of artistic invention (a possibility Guston realized and mentioned later in a letter to Berkson).

Although a professional independence and distance is kept by each figure through the separate pages that contain their work, the net result is that the blend of talents erases a primary voice. No controlling ego or intellect overwhelms the combinations. While these were effects that Guston never consciously entertained or sought at the time (at least not as he revealed himself through statements and correspondence), they nonetheless would become vital ingredients of his *Poem-Pictures* and the myriad interactions he would sustain with writers in the 1970s.

Bill Berkson was an essential catalyst in engineering many of Guston's introductions to poets after 1967–68. Berkson (who has a dual life as a poet and writer on art) had met Guston in New York in the early 1960s and had written about his abstractions with insight and enthusiasm for various magazines. The dramatic resurfacing of imagery in the artist's drawings in the late 1960s— the immediacy of the drawing process first caught the figures and objects which would later flood Guston's painting—was a development with which Berkson required no reckoning. Unlike Guston's many defectors, Berkson read the meaning of the change both for its audacity and inevitability. On the eve of his exhibition at the Marlborough Gallery in 1970, Guston wrote to Berkson:

> I'm very excited by your comments—"Energy, Vision" etc. about the new work—and of course I agree about an "Art World" we both seem to be quite through with and don't know how to think about at all. But, I think that is what will be exhilarating about showing this work now— at this time. I mean its very remoteness from the elegant fashion environmental art. Oh well you know what I mean. I've been feeling for so long now about what it makes me want to paint—it is to tell a story—to put in a picture (and not leave out anything!) what I've always wanted to see but hadn't until now, for the first time. And not find out in process or anything like that—no "self identity," no "discoveries," no "purities"—just (but) images of places, atmospheres, things— recognition of long forgotten places. It's as if I've made a leap over a heap of dead bodies of notions and ideas—and landed in a new air of clarity and precision—does an artist ever really know what he does?[13]

Berkson, who by this point also felt the need for some distance from New York, had relocated to the San Francisco area. However, he kept up and perhaps even intensified his relationship with Guston through a similar interest in redirecting his work. Prior to his move to the West Coast, Berkson put Guston in touch with a number of poets, including Clark Coolidge, Anne Waldman, and Lewis Warsh, all of whom visited the artist in Woodstock at various times and who identified with the content of his new painting. Berkson recalls first seeing the late imagery in 1969 with Waldman and Warsh. They made the visit to Woodstock to entice Guston to produce a cover for the book of Coolidge's poem, *ING* (a publication of Angel Hair Press, which was run by Waldman and Warsh):

> . . . when we got to the studio those drawings were always somewhere and there were small boards stacked up—luscious cartoon-like paintings of common objects (clocks) and some not-so common of the hooded figures brandishing their little whips. . . . A

kind of haphazard theatricality took hold, everybody rushing dizzily from wall to wall collaborating with Guston on his "story," identifying incidents and figures or just sitting stunned on stools contemplating all this unfathomable energy.[14]

Coolidge, who accompanied Berkson on another studio visit the following year, saw the new work as a continuation, a logical sequel to the formal contradictions posited in his abstractions:

> Spent hours talking about his hundreds of new paintings in giant
> new studio out back. First glimpse I had of them I couldn't resist
> exclaiming: 'R. Crumb!' Piles of cars, and shoes, and clocks, & Ku-Klux-
> Klanners (and books) all merged into that patented Guston-center,
> except all those shapes from the mid-1950s (ever think how the mid-
> '50s contained simultaneously: The Coasters, The Penguins, and Fats
> Domino and Presley and all of them plus Pollock, Kline, de Kooning,
> Guston et al?)[15]

This kind of reading, which was expansive in its assessment of culture, which made linkages and parallels between the arts without the bias of high-minded assumptions about the purity of abstract painting (assumptions that Guston himself once upheld), appealed to the artist's reconstructed view of art.

Berkson's move to the Bay area did not limit his contact with Guston. An extensive correspondence was struck (much of which now appears one-sided as Guston retained few of Berkson's letters). Some of Guston's letters centered on the drawings that he gave to Berkson for the covers and interiors of two issues of *BIG SKY*, the publication that Berkson edited, as well as for *Enigma Variations*. Guston dwells in these letters on the resemblance and unity of interest which existed between his and Berkson's new work. These resemblances spawned Guston's effusive analysis, in addition to the first *Poem-Pictures*:

> NOW, NEGATIVE, is absolutely marvelous—right up my alley, as they
> say—like a Kafka aphorism in that it never finishes itself with the
> thought, but is "circular," endlessly in movement. Too, what you are left
> with is not the "thought," but a sense of forces, "abstract" powers, but
> yet again one comes back to the thought AND THINGS. It goes on and
> on—and also so mysterious—the word "restaurant" is wonderful, where
> it is "restaurant closes"—Well, it's an inspired nugget—Both A-FRAME &
> CANTO, went like a breeze for me, as I drew—In a word, I "FEEL" the new
> work, they are just wonderful and I want to tell you, you are doing the
> "best" writing now. The drawings are my way of telling you that.[16]

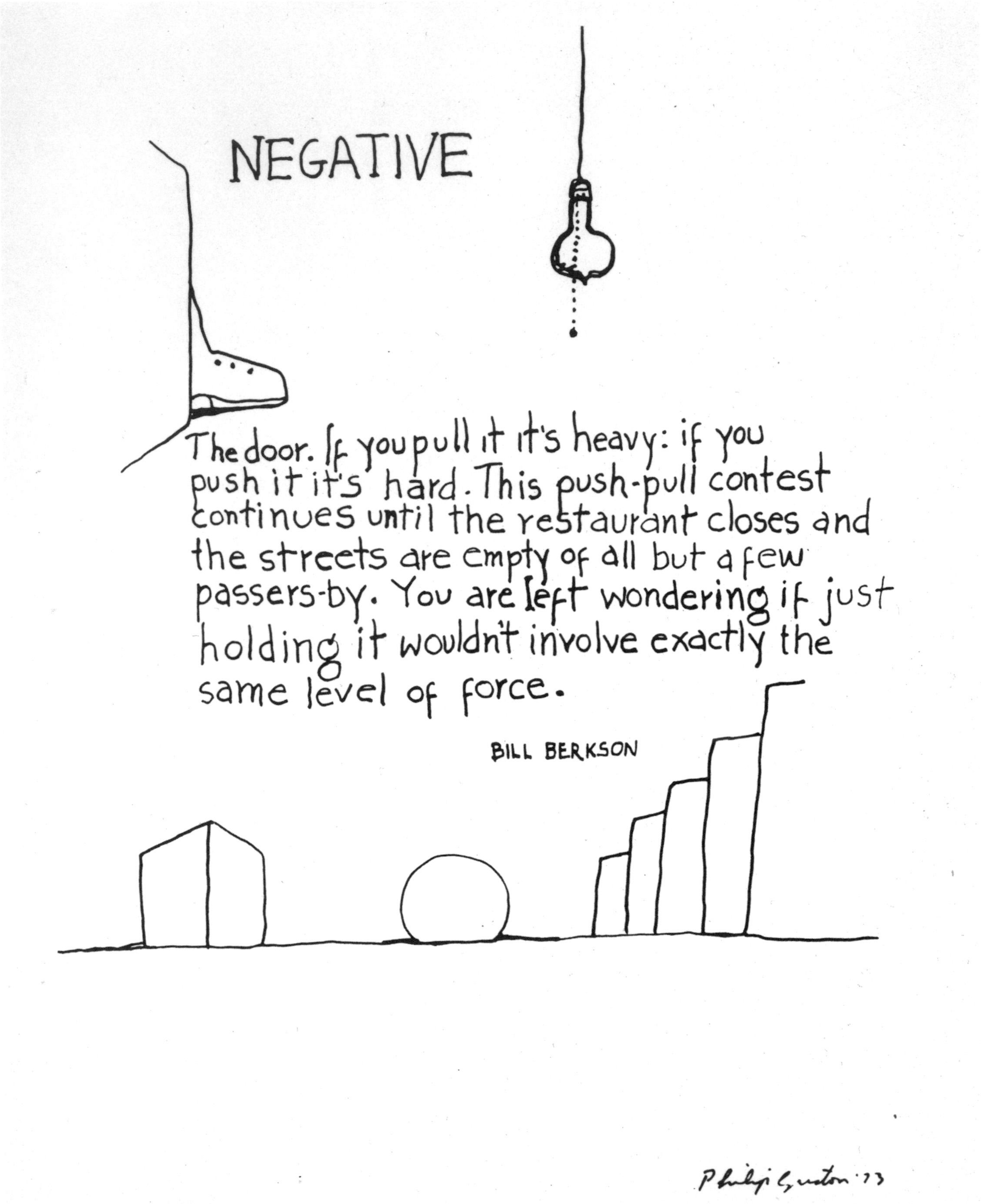

NEGATIVE

The door. If you pull it it's heavy: if you push it it's hard. This push-pull contest continues until the restaurant closes and the streets are empty of all but a few passers-by. You are left wondering if just holding it wouldn't involve exactly the same level of force.

BILL BERKSON

Philip Guston '73

PLATE 8

22

The drawings were unexpected, a surprise, a genuine outpouring of admiration. Berkson was moved by the tribute:

> Philip GOOD GOD!!! The Perfect Tube Arrives. You certainly know how
> to deliver, & I am bowled over! All three drawings make a connection
> direct from you to me, and (I must presume) back to you, but in a way
> that the notion of "feedback" is hardly equal to.... More like a "click" so
> simultaneous as to (in 2 places) be one event. Well, I don't really know
> about that but I do know I love it & love (and thank) you for it.[17]

Negative (pl. 8), *CANTO*, and *A-FRAME*, as Berkson states, are "one event," a fusion of text and image. Unlike *Enigma Variations*, in which a page of writing is placed opposite to a page with a picture, where no visual overlap occurs, the poems are integrated with drawings on a single sheet of paper and read as a unit. While only vague correspondences exist between the drawing and poem, the two are unified through a common intent to realize a state of ambiguity or some conundrum through the mingling of mutually exclusive ideas. Ordinary things such as a hanging light bulb and a shoe that protrudes through a door (the single literal reference to the poem) are brought into contact with a line-up of geometric shapes such as a circle, cube, and a row of squares, all of which pick up on the elusive or "mysterious," as Guston put it, meaning of the poem. Any attempt at illustration here, would throw the match of interests off balance, let alone be near-impossible to picture given the conceptual nature of the text. Besides, the drawing would also become subservient to the poem. As it is, an artistic equivalence is achieved. No one's work overrides or dominates the other's. The drawings of Berkson's poems emerge as a prelude to the *Poem-Pictures*. As a group, the *Poem-Pictures* number somewhere in excess of one hundred drawings, all of which were executed sometime in and around 1975–76.[18] With the dwindled critical reception to Guston's late work (something that would not escalate again until the end of the decade when a substantial following developed for his painting) and the alienation he felt from the New York School of artists, he became increasingly more at home in the company of writers. They seemed to exert bearing on or at least reinforcement for many of the ideas with which he was absorbed in his studio. In a letter to Berkson in 1973, Guston wrote:

> I saw Lewis [Warsh] in Boston, he came to my little slide talk—
> monologue—It was lovely seeing him, talking to him.... Met other
> poets in Detroit—seems to be a widespread network of the new
> poetry—How wonderful—makes me want to paint and draw forever.[19]

Similarly, on his burgeoning friendship with Coolidge, he wrote, "He's terrific to be with— I always feel an excitement—a relevancy—and he sees things in a special close way. I am lucky to have him near and know him."[20]

The *Poem-Pictures*, the tangible outgrowth of all of this conversation and comradery, comprise a salient dimension of Guston's late work. The number of drawings alone that grew out of his exchanges and friendships with poets speaks of the significance that Guston attached to this body of work. As Guston's declarations reveal in letters to Berkson, the coupling of words and images presented a new area of invention, possibilities for adding to the already prolific imagery of his late work. But the collision of language and picture in these drawings also engages (not so unwittingly on Guston's part) a number of intriguing aesthetic issues, which steer an interpretation of the final phase of his work beyond the discourse of modernism, with all its idealization of originality and authorship, signature terms that most writers have brought to bear on Guston's career.

The *Poem-Pictures* fall into a number of distinct groupings, the most obvious being those clustered around the work of each poet. Each collaboration—a description used in the metaphoric sense since the *Poem-Pictures* did not evolve from actual dialogue or mutual decision-making—has its own distinct identity, a feature that suggests none of these drawings were arbitrary accompaniments to poems. They were, in fact, tailored to the tone and content of each piece of writing. Following the three drawings that Guston made in 1973, which incorporated Berkson's poems, a spate of work surfaced that more fully formed the corpus of *Poem-Pictures*. This thematic entity consists, in addition to work by Berkson, of collaborative exchanges with Coolidge, McKim, and Corbett as well as with Stanley Kunitz, an old friend whom Guston had known since the 1950s.

Again the chronology that defines the unfolding of these drawings falls somewhere around 1975–76. Moreover, as considerable overlap seems to surround Guston's various projects with writers, no coherent sorting by date and order can be made of this work. A letter from Guston to Bill Corbett in October, 1975, alludes to an absence of plan, a spontaneous generation of all of the *Poem-Pictures*:

> I've done a sizable group of drawings for your poems. I'll bring them up to
> show you and hope they appeal to you. I've taken poems of yours that
> appealed to me greatly and gave me an immediate response in terms of
> imagery. Clark, who was here last weekend, thought they were fine and
> urges me to bring them to you. I've done a large group of his poems too,
> as well as Musa's—Bill Berkson has quite a number of drawings of his work.
> The past couple of weeks has been poem-drawings instead of painting—
> When I get the call—is the best way of doing them of course.[21]

However capricious the origins of these drawings might seem, something other than impulse triggered their ideation. Certainly, Guston's use of Berkson's poems set the process in motion. Coolidge, a figure who became an important and valued friend to Guston in the last decade of his life, has described the activity, or what sounds vaguely like a program, that went

figure 2. Bill Berkson and Philip Guston at Paule Anglim Gallery, San Franciso, Jan. 6, 1979.
Photo courtesy Bill Berkson.

figure 3. Musa McKim and Philip Guston, Woodstock, New York. Photo courtesy Renée McKee.

into his *Poem-Pictures*. His account reveals Guston had some strategy or method in mind to embody Coolidge's poetry in his work:

> I would send him poems. He had carte blanche to do whatever he wanted. I don't remember ever actually telling him that, but that was understood. Usually the way we would work is he would call up, and he would have a lot of painting he would want to talk about. I would go to Woodstock and spend a couple of days. After that, I would come back and feel incredibly energetic and just want to write. I would usually send him that work. This process fed back and forth between us. Then, he would make drawings; he was always making drawings. He would take out a line of my poetry that he liked. Although some are complete poems, we never sat down together and did them. It was always that I would send them to him. We're both pretty solitary workers. [22]

Coolidge's *Poem-Pictures* are by far the largest of Guston's collaborations with writers, numbering in the vicinity of forty drawings and one painting. While the sheer volume of material that grew out of their exchanges is partly explained by the proximity of their homes and the frequency of their visits—Coolidge moved from San Francisco to the Berkshires in 1970, three years after Guston set up permanent residence in Woodstock—a deeper connection animated their friendship. Coolidge, almost twenty years younger than Guston, was someone whom the artist would come to refer to by the mid 1970s (the period of the *Poem-Pictures*) as a "beautiful man,"[23] with "a very good eye and a sharply analytic mind."[24] He came to trust and even rely upon Coolidge's aesthetic judgement, a dependence that grew out of their common enthusiasm for writers such as Herman Melville, Franz Kafka, and Samuel Beckett. "Philip was a very literate guy, for a painter," Coolidge recalls. "He wasn't like most painters. He read because he loved to read. He was literate, in the sense that he read heavy literature."[25]

In the many night-long discussions that Coolidge and Guston held in the artist's studio, Guston would encourage the poet to convey any instant reaction he might have to Guston's new work: "He loved to have me say whatever came into my mind," Coolidge said. "He was in love with the poet's mind. I'm sure it was such a fresh antidote to the art world."[26] Coolidge's *Poem-Pictures* are saturated with the immediacy of these conversations. In collaborations such as *.....The Space Between Things* (pl. 6), *... I am the first to Have Seen Where I Live* (pl. 23), and *Lines, Drops* (pl. 22) the broken narratives, fractured sentences, and discontinuous words and threads of thoughts, parallel the type of visual fissures that Guston was attempting to effect in his own work. Guston excerpted from Coolidge's poems (few complete poems appear in these drawings), a fact that heightens the sense of fragmentation in the poet's work. Some of the images in these drawings are tied to specific words and lines of poetry. For example, in *... Smoking and Drawing* (pl. 16) two of Guston's now trademark Cyclops-type heads appear, one holds a burning cigarette while another eyes a pencil. The passage that Guston has pulled from Coolidge's poem is neatly correlated with his imagery:

... Smoking and Drawing,

Both Thoughts of Another Finger

Circles, Both Time and Light, Enough

For All Stops On One Line ...

The kind of visual/verbal balance that is attained in this juxtaposition runs through many of the Guston/Coolidge *Poem-Pictures*. In .. *The Painter Can't Sleep for Sight Won't Move* (cover) an eyeball (a literal representation of sight) is combined with three paint-brushes (emblems of the painter's craft) while more allusive depictions of an aged tree sprouting new leaves and the full sun occupy the center of the compositional space. Some arcane reading of stasis and regeneration, could be coaxed from this mingling of elements, caught as all of this cryptic imagery is in Guston's own personal history; but, illustration or pictorial embellishment of a poem is one thing that the collaborative team of Guston and Coolidge did not have in mind. For as many of the *Poem-Pictures* with cross-overs between image and text, there exist an equal number with little or no internal relationship. Compare, for instance, ... *Borderlands* (pl. 37) and .. *The Heart of Weight* in which no correspondence of word and picture exists. As Coolidge stated as early as 1967, at the time Guston was approached by Berkson to produce the cover for Coolidge's *ING*:

> Been doing a lot of thought on Book Covers and Their nature and Problems
> for the Writer (and Artist) and I finally think ... there's probably little or no
> connection between the cover and the innards, nor should there be,
> directly. Better some kind of friendly antagonism or spark-gap. Otherwise
> you get some kind of illustration situation or Pik of the writer.... Actually
> even if somebody thought of "illustrating" they'd be operating at quite a
> distance or giving false-leads (like imagine a cover for ING being a picture of
> dictionary-page fragments scattered around a room and somebody seeing
> say hmmm), so THAT'S what he's all about! and goes on to read the book,
> getting only one dimension the while, or a photograph (imagine an edition
> of the Bible with a cover-pik of Jesus sitting in his underwear, a rack of tools
> on the walls just behind him) ... [27]

Admittedly a difference obtains between the cover for *ING* (with its recto and verso images of vertical lines, a representation that hardly restates the book's "innards") and all of the ensuing *Poem-Pictures*. *ING* is a book cover, after all, a genre that retains a natural aesthetic distance from the contents within. No concrete interaction between artist and poet takes place in the project. Moreover, the combination of Coolidge and Guston in this volume was engineered by an intermediary, the publisher,[28] with the result that any suggestion of a creative totality is by happenstance, undetermined by each figure. As Coolidge explains above, illustration or even synthesis was not the objective in *ING*. Surely, some of the same intentions apply to the *Poem-Pictures*. Although Coolidge and Guston were quite consciously picking up on many of the descriptions and figures in each other's work—the references to smoking and drawing, among other lines in

Coolidge's poems, also reify the talk and events of their evenings—the aim in their collaborations was to realize as much semantic and compositional rupture as possible without the collaboration disintegrating into complete disorder. What Guston and Coolidge shared, then, was a common aesthetic that valued the *non sequitur* or discontinuous image, word, or phrase over any linear, logical, or straightforward development of a story.

That Guston extracted lines and portions of Coolidge's poems in his drawings, disassembled their unity, sets them apart from the *Poem-Pictures* he produced for Musa McKim, William Corbett, and Stanley Kunitz. All of the work that Guston produced for these figures incorporated whole poems, or at least, intact stanzas. The difference of approach can be construed by the more lyrical style of these poets whose writing could not be as easily broken into sections, structured as they are around a theme and a temporal dimension. Guston's drawings interestingly adjust to these poems' more descriptive modes of expression. In fact, the artist frequently makes quite literal translations of the content of these various poems. For instance, in McKim's *Awakened by a Mosquito in the Villa Aurelia* (pl. 31), Guston depicts the setting of the poem with considerable specificity. The geography or particulars of the place, in this case the city of Rome, are rendered with versimilitude (albeit with the distinctive rawness of Guston's late style). Taking his cue from the line "… by the terrace with a view of half of Rome …," Guston's picture follows with quasi-fidelity the architectural highlights of this built environment: the dome of St. Peter's dominates the foreground of the scene, which has been perched in the upper half of the drawing so as to convey some sense of a vista or "view." The same kind of visual re-enactment occurs in William

figure 4. Philip Guston, Stanley Kunitz, *1959. Photo courtesy Stanley Kunitz.*

Corbett's *The Richard Nixon Story* (pl. 26). A towering and unmistakable caricature of Nixon, decrepit and miserable, his left foot inflamed with phlebitis, overwhelms the surface of the drawing. About two-thirds of Corbett's poem is splayed diagonally along the back of Nixon's body with the concluding lines spread horizontally over the waters of "Key Biscayne and San Clemente." The relationship between word and image could not be more direct or even.

A similar affinity exists in Guston's *Poem-Picture* of Stanley Kunitz's *Vita Nuova* (pl. 1). Although metaphysical in nature, the onto-logical ponderings of this poem are not lost on Guston's interpretation. For the following stanza of Kunitz's work, Guston has delved into his repertoire of late images and found the appropriate counterparts:

Moon of the soul accompany me now,
Shine on the colosseums of my sense,
Be in the tabernacles of my brow.
My dark will make, reflecting from your stones,
The single beam of all my life intense.

In this painting, a medium that Guston rarely used for the *Poem-Pictures*, one of Guston's Cyclops-type heads muses on the lines (or perhaps "beam") which emanate from his fingers while the full moon hovers above. Like the poem, the image is allegorical, a reverie on the trajectory of the soul.

MORE CASES AGAINST ILLUSTRATION

Corbett has raised, within the context of his own *Poem-Pictures*, the whole issue of illustration (the now recurring differentiation that cuts through all of this material). On the question of Guston's intent, Corbett has written:

> I say "draw" rather than illustrated because I do not see Guston as making a picture
> to go with a poem. He seemed to draw out the poem images as a reader does. As
> he wrote out the words of the poem in his hand his act seems that much closer
> to reading than illustration, to discovering the poem for himself.[29]

To buttress this claim, Corbett has noted "In the case of *12 April* I know the drawing came before the poem. It is, empty of poem, in the background of a photograph in Dore Ashton's book on Guston *Yes, But...*"[30]

Coolidge has also traced a few of his *Poem-Pictures* to pre-existing drawings through reproductions in Ashton's book.[31] These exceptions add to the case against illustration (as Corbett argues), against any inclination to dismiss Guston's imagery as mere accessories of the poems. Conversely, the later addition of words to drawings in no way diminishes the case for collaboration. The physical evidence alone of poem and picture coupled on one page or sheet of drawing paper, however, after the fact, attests to some attempt to bring about a creative merger. In *12 April* the amalgamation of poem and imagery both alter and enhance their original meanings. This collaboration, like all the others, is a composite, a hybrid work of art that remains disaffected of any desire towards hierarchy, aesthetic purity, or the projection of one figure's individuality or ego on the other's work.

Whatever the actual outcome, Guston clearly had the upper hand in these exchanges. The poems that were incorporated into these drawings were, after all, Guston's selection. We know from Coolidge's recollections that the two discussed their collaboration in a nominal sense. However, the Guston/Coolidge exchange operated primarily on a conceptual level, with the artist being given "carte blanche," as Coolidge put it, to rummage freely through his poetry for lines and phrases that were best suited to the artist's new work. Moreover, this process took place from afar and without Coolidge's active participation.

The circumstances that frame the production of *Poem-Pictures* for Berkson, McKim, Corbett, and Kunitz are even more concealed and private. While no statements have surfaced that refer to the occasions that surround Guston's drawings of McKim's poems (their domestic partnership suggests that more complex feelings stratified their collaborations), the *Poem-Pictures* that grew out of Guston's exchanges with Berkson, Corbett, and Kunitz were all surprises, underscoring a lack of direct input from the poets.

The drawings of Corbett's poems evolved in much the same way as Berkson's. Corbett, who wrote *Columbus Square Journal* (pl. 9), a book of poetry, also asked Guston (who from 1973 to 1977 commuted from Woodstock to teach at Boston University), to design a cover for the publication. The request led to Corbett's *Poem-Pictures*:

> In May of 1977, I opened a package from him. It took one moment to realize that in each of seven cover drawings he titled the book *Columbus Square Journal*. [Corbett had originally given the manuscript the title of *Columbus Day a Year*, which Guston took the liberty of altering.] Perfect.... That Fall Philip arrived for dinner with another larger package. For this he took a dozen drawings of poems for the book. Although I knew he had "drawn" poems by his wife, and by Clark Coolidge and Bill Berkson, I was flabbergasted and honored to see this evidence of the attention he had paid to my work.[32]

Stanley Kunitz experienced the same kind of overture:

> In 1976, when I was Consultant in Poetry to the Library of Congress, the Smithsonian Institution commissioned him, in collaboration with me, to design a poster celebrating the marriage of poetry and painting. The poster that he executed, in his late brutal style, incorporating some of my lines, was an extraordinary work, so powerful in fact that it succeeded in frightening the people at the Smithsonian. As part of our contract, Philip and I had agreed to conduct a public dialogue in Washington, but the event was canceled on the eve. "Bastards!" cried Philip. "They think they can treat us like a pair of old farts!" And then, as if to compensate for our failed expectations, he made a beautiful gesture, presenting me with the original painting—oil on paper—together with a set of magnificent drawings based on other poems of mine that he favored. These are treasures.[33]

That Guston initiated these various exchanges, that he assumed the position of authority by culling what he wanted from the work of poets, makes these collaborations considerably one-sided, tilted in his favor. But are they? The use of the word collaboration throughout this essay is and continues to be in the "metaphoric" sense, meaning that these drawings represent an alliance of talents, a shift away from the modernist emphasis on "originality" and its straight jacket of "self-expression." To characterize the *Poem-Pictures* as "tributes" or "homages" seems too easy, too willing to pass this material off as miscellaneous, a minor incident in the larger scheme of Guston's work. The details of these collaborations, that is, the way in which they were made, implies Guston was the dominant intellect. The context of Guston's interactions with writers in the last decade of his life, however, suggests something quite different.

PLATE 9

Literature had always occupied a central place in Guston's life. As a young artist in Los Angeles, he met (and read) Nathaniel West and a number of screen writers through the artist Fletcher Martin. These literary associations were essential to Guston, ones that he not only sought throughout his career, but upon which he became increasingly dependent. There was something nurturing about the company of writers to Guston. On his relationship with Robert Phelps, a writer with whom Guston was particularly close from 1947 through 1956 (a period in which his earlier figurative work moved towards an abstract style), he said, "Robert was often in my studio, seeing those early struggles of the fifties and was, to me, great moral support. More importantly, his wide reading of modern literature and criticism was important to me."[34] Morton Feldman, the composer, was also someone who Guston "saw … almost daily, talking and talking about art and ideas constantly,"[35] from around 1950 to 1970. Other figures, such as Stanley Kunitz and Bill Berkson, also filled the literary spaces of his world. And one cannot discount Musa, who while shy and seemingly invisible, in the background in her role as a wife, must have also exerted influence (undoubtably more subliminal) through her capacity as a poet, an occupation she approached with modesty.[36]

"I always like to be equipped to be in the company of writers. When you read a man you are in contact with his mind," Guston has said.[37] As Coolidge has recounted, Guston was an insatiable reader. From Phelps, he was introduced to literary figures such as Colette, Henry Green, Genet, Auden, Rilke, and Marcel Jouhandeau.[38] Kunitz steered their conversations towards poets such as Gerald Manley Hopkins and William Butler Yeats.[39] Later, especially as his painting became immersed in abstract expressionism, Sartre, Camus, and Beckett, the authors of alienation and anxiety, became preoccupations. The Russians—Dostoyevsky, Gogol, Chekhov, and Pasternak—were also ongoing literary pursuits throughout the 1950s, as their writing was given to the moral dimension of existence, an area that Guston believed drove his own work.[40]

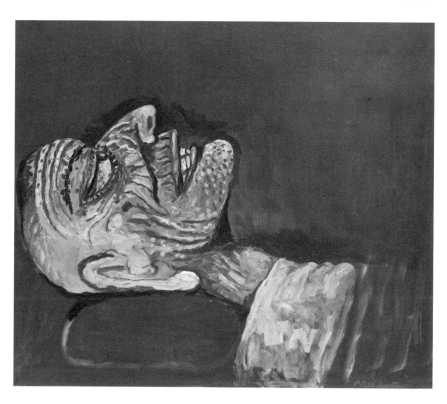

figure 5. Philip Guston, East Coker-TSE, 1979, oil on canvas, 42 x 49".
The Museum of Modern Art, New York. Gift of Musa Guston.

Yet Kafka, Kierkegaard, and Babel were recurring literary exemplars to Guston, writers whose work most resembled his own interests, whatever the moment or juncture of his varied stylistic output. Their sense of irony (particularly in the writing of Kafka), and construction of dialectical relationships, were enormously appealing to Guston, especially in their uncovering of the world of appearances and the different, frequently more startling realities beneath. On Kafka and Babel, he expounded at the end of his life, after years of reading and re-reading their work:

> I was thinking one night about Kafka's story, "The Metamorphosis,"
> when he wakes up and he's a bug and he's late for work. Well, I think
> the most fantastic thing about this story is that this man has not
> really changed. He's totally conscious, totally aware. There's no meta-
> morphosis. I like Isaac Babel too because he deals totally with fact.[41]

During the 1950s, Guston began dedicating many of his paintings to writers and artists. The beneficiaries of this practice include Bradley Walker Tomlin, Fellini, Kierkegaard, Morton Feldman, T.S. Eliot (fig. 5), Isaac Babel, Ross Feld, and Musa, among others. These dedications emerge as a catalogue of Guston's meandering cultural interests. They outline the shape of his reading and artistic encounters, as well as enumerate some of the names that floated in and out of the conversations he conducted with his literary companions in the 1970s. In the last few years of his life, these inscriptions—which took the form of initialing the muse's name somewhere on the canvas, for example: "To J.S. 1977" (Jules Supervielle)—accelerated, a penchant that mirrors Guston's heightened reliance on writers.

Guston stated just before his death, "The few people who visit me are poets or writers, rather than painters, because I value their reactions."[42] One of the ingredients of these interactions that he found so compelling (to revisit a theme posited at the beginning of this essay) was the kind of unencumbered, theory-free descriptions that poets and writers brought to his work. On Coolidge, whose responses were always prized by Guston, he remarked:

> Looking at this painting [this statement is not annotated, hence the
> specific work is unknown], Clark Coolidge . . . said that it looked as if an
> invisible presence had been there, but had left these objects and gone
> somewhere else. I like that kind of reaction, compared with reactions like
> the green works, the blue doesn't work.[43]

Coolidge was someone whom Guston compared to Robert Phelps, someone, as he described "with whom there is . . . an involved artistic relationship, with whom I can discuss whatever is on my mind regarding my work and disturbing painting problems."[44]

The radical juxtapositions of incongruous figures and objects in his late paintings, all of which engage aspects of Guston's biography, were rendered with the artist's great apprehension and doubt. The outpouring of images in his work around 1967–68, the KKK (hooded figures that he thought of as self-portraits), books, hanging light bulbs, and clocks, among other things, combined with the unsettling implications of this new work, both in terms of the painful stirring of Guston's childhood memories as well as for the overall state of abstract art, made for a situation that required extra bolstering from friends. Philip Roth, who rented a cabin in Woodstock in 1969 shortly after the huge success of his *Portnoy's Complaint*, and who became another literary friend, remembers Guston's ambivalence and insecurity about the development of this imagery:

> At fifty-six, he was twenty years older than I and full of the doubts and uncertainties that can beset an artist of consequence in late middle age. He felt that he'd exhausted the means that previously had unlocked him as an abstract painter, and was bored and disgusted by the skills that had gained him renown. He didn't want to paint like that ever again; somedays he even tried to convince himself that he shouldn't paint at all. But since nothing but painting could contain his emotional turbulence, let alone begin to deplete his self-mythologizing monomania, renouncing painting would have been tantamount to committing suicide or, at the very least, have meant burying himself alive in that coffin clinically described as depression.[45]

Guston's relationship to abstract painting, even at the height of his commitment to metaphysical issues, was at best uneasy. As early as 1958, eight or nine years before the wild mix of figures and objects surfaced in his work, he was to question what gains, if any, had been made by the ascendancy of vanguard art: "I do not see why the loss of faith in the known image and symbol in our time should be celebrated as a freedom. It is a loss from which we suffer, and this pathos motivates modern painting and poetry at its heart."[46] Guston was a relatively late convert to the enterprise of abstract expression. His entry into the domain of "Action Painting" (as his friend the critic Harold Rosenberg called it) around 1947 came about more slowly and lagged behind Jackson Pollock, Mark Rothko, and others, who got to the forefront as early as 1943. This detail suggests a reluctance to forego figuration, as well as a belief in its power to produce universal meaning. Even when Guston became fully involved in the speculative venture of abstract painting, he would always defend the case for representational art: "The trouble with most modern painting is that it's too clear. The painting of the past which fascinates me is the painting which you can spend the rest of your life trying to figure out, trying to fathom what the artist's intentions were."[47]

By the end of his career, Guston, long after his stint as an abstract painter was over, had become thoroughly agitated on the subject of modernist art:

> There is something ridiculous and miserly in the myth we inherit from abstract art.... That painting is autonomous, pure and for itself, and therefore we habitually define its ingredients and define its limits. But

painting is "impure." It is the adjustment of impurities which forces painting's continuity. "We are image-makers and image-ridden."[48]

The critical reception and limited audience to Guston's late work no doubt fed his mocking of the New York School. He was acting out, venting his feelings of anger and betrayal. The derisive language that Hilton Kramer and others in the press employed to undermine Guston's new paintings had stuck throughout the decade of the 1970s. While a certain show of sympathy from critics and artists co-existed alongside of this sneering, Guston was frequently undone by the cruelty of these reviews. An exhibition at McKee Gallery, New York in 1974 rekindled the suffering he experienced earlier in 1970:

> [I am] ... in a state of depression—(momentarily, I hope) reading reviews, articles on the show—Personal attacks—"my desire towards suicide," "compared to De Sade"—or "I'm a cartoonist" and on and on—(My God, am I paranoid?) right now I wonder if I can weather the storm. Poor Clark—*Bless him*—was here a couple of weeks ago, when I was in the middle of all this flack and mis-understanding and his presence and talk helped me considerably (how *weak* we all are, after all).[49]

Only his circle of poets and writers (which included, of course, Musa) could relieve Guston's enormous anxiety.

The *Poem-Pictures* are surely part of this context. They emanate from a need for union, to fix his new artistic allegiances in some material form. The double signatures that appear in these drawings subjugate or decentralize a single authorial or artistic voice. Guston, for the first time in his career, shared the white space of his drawing paper with somebody else. It took a crisis of faith, a deep realization that the modernist model of "purity" (to use one of his words), with all its emphasis on originality and the self-sufficiency of art, no longer served him. Moreover, the integration of image and text in the *Poem-Pictures* neutralizes the issue of subjectivity. While Guston's late work has generally been construed as the final outburst of his considerable ego, the end point of a romantic "voyage"[50] into self-expression, these composite drawings counter this reading. Their existence suggests that a more open, inconclusive, and heterogeneous approach to art informed Guston's revised aesthetic outlook. The imprint of another mind on his work is a sign of an interest in altering the prevailing canon of art, to move beyond modernism's primary investment in the unique personality.

Like the piles of objects (shards of civilization) in *Hill Side*, 1979, the bandaged head in *Untitled*, 1980, or the blood-shot eyes of the artist with his burning cigarette and bottle of alcohol in *The Painter*, 1976, Guston's late work—of which the *Poem-Pictures* are an important part—can be seen as allegories for the ruin or collapse of modernism and its rigid prescription for the origination of individual styles and new forms. Guston's aim in his paintings and drawings from 1967–68 onwards was to be "more inclusive rather than exclusive," as he phrased it,[51] to unveil himself and the world around him, as well as to spurn the hidden identities that had cloistered abstract painting for so long.

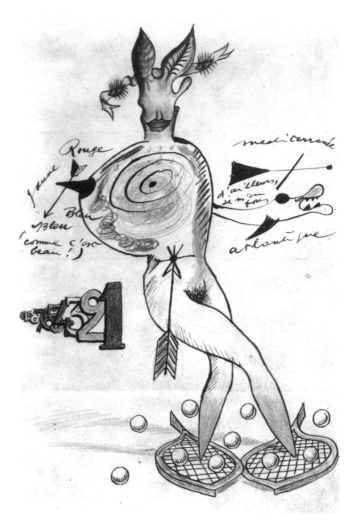

figure 7. Cadavre Exquis, Figure, 1926–27, pen and ink, pencil, and crayon, 14 ⅛ x 9". By (top to bottom) Yves Tanguy, Joan Miro, Max Morisse, Man Ray. The Museum of Modern Art, New York. Purchase Fund.

figure 6. Sonia Delaunay-Terk, Decoration for La Prose du Transsiberien et da la Petite Jehanne de France, by Blaise Cendrars, Paris, Editions des Hommes Nouveaux, 1913, Pochoir, printed in color, scroll, sheet: 81 ½ x 13 ⅞", The Museum of Modern Art, New York. Purchase.

figure 8. Norman Bluhm and Frank O'Hara, Hand, (from 22 Poem Paintings), 1960, gouache on paper, 14 x 19¼", Grey Art Gallery & Study Center, New York University Art Collection. Gift of the artist, 1966. Photo by Charles Uht.

The *Poem-Pictures* are part of an ongoing and extensive twentieth-century practice of artistic collaboration. Sonia Delaunay-Terk's and Blaise Cendrars's *La prose du Transsiberien et la Petite Jehanne de France*, 1913 (fig. 6), a long pochoir scroll printed in color which pairs a poem with quasi-Cubist shapes is generally assumed to be one of the first attempts at an artist/poet merger. Later, after intermittent activity, the *Cadavre Exquise* (fig. 7), the Surrealist version of the Victorian parlor game, became a popular collaborative genre in the late 1920s and early 1930s. A sheet of paper folded in three or four sections was passed to various participants to draw, in sequential order, areas of the human anatomy. When opened, a hybrid creature emerged, the outcome of their multiple sensitivities. By the time Norman Bluhm and Frank O'Hara teamed up to produce their *22 Poem Paintings*, 1960 (fig. 8), a fusion of paint and text, a rich and complex history of collaborations existed. Some of the highlights of this history also include the photomontage collaborations of George Grosz, Raoul Hausmann, Hannah Hoch, and John Heartfield of c. 1917–20, the many duo drawings by Sophie Taueber and Hans Arp from 1918 through the 1940s, as well as the "cut-ups" of William Burroughs and Bryon Gysin from the 1960s, whose collaboration took the form of shredding their writing and reconfiguring it in varying patterns on a page.

Trivialized by most interpreters of the culture of modernism as marginal, inconsequential, and most of all as mere fun (the inherited fate of Guston's *Poem-Pictures*), these joint projects confound our traditionally received notions of art. Whatever the composition of the collaborative duo or team, be they a pair or group of artists, or of a mix of artists and writers, or even dancers and musicians, the bias against their exchanges have remained the same. Their combined efforts have been measured by a set of standards that presupposes that art is a pure enterprise, the outgrowth of isolation and solitary thinking.

Guston was undoubtably familiar with much of this history. He had befriended Frank O'Hara around 1960 and must have known of the poet's many collaborations with artists such as Grace Hartigan, Larry Rivers, Jasper Johns, and Joe Brainard in addition to Bluhm. Guston referred to O'Hara as "our Apollinaire."[52] When The Museum of Modern Art gathered together a collection of prints by artists to accompany poems by O'Hara as a tribute after his death, Guston was one of the contributors. The volume, known as *In Memory of My Feelings* (pl. 10) after a title from one of O'Hara's poems, consists primarily of separate pages of text and image placed in apposition, an arrangement that differs from his projects with Bluhm and others. An elegiac collaboration? Or, an acknowledgement of or reply to his work? If situated only within the context of commemoration, the prints that comprise this book would seem doomed to decoration, a mere appendage to O'Hara's work. O'Hara provided the answer in advance of his death. His poem *WHY I AM NOT A PAINTER* alludes to the mutually subtle influences and points of contact that grow out of his artistic exchanges and friendships:

I am not a painter. I am a poet.
Why? I think I would rather be
a painter, but I am not. Well,
for instance, Mike Goldberg
is starting a painting. I drop in.
"Sit down and have a drink he
says. I drink; we drink. I look
up. "You have SARDINES in it."
"Yes, it needed something there."
"Oh." I go and the days go by
and I drop in again. The painting
is going on, and I go, and the days
go by. I drop in. The painting is
finished. "Where's SARDINES?"
All that's left is just letters.
"It was too much," Mike says.

But me? One day I am thinking of
a color: orange. I write a line
about orange. Pretty soon it is a
whole page of words, not lines.
Then another page. There should be
so much more, not of orange, of
words, of how terrible orange is
and life. Days go by. It is even in
prose, I am a real poet. My poem
is finished and I haven't mentioned
orange yet. It's twelve poems, I call
it ORANGES. And one day in the gallery
I see Mike's painting, called SARDINES.[53]

All of the prints in *In Memory of My Feelings* are the work of O'Hara's friends. Their ideas had already delicately marked his poems. The book can be seen as a synthesis, then, the sum of his creative existence.

Guston's *Poem-Pictures* are an apt comparison to O'Hara's interactions with artists. Not only do they approach the scope and number of O'Hara's collaborations, but a similar necessity to effect a union with another artistic or literary figure motivates Guston's drawings of poems.

Did the *Poem-Pictures* alter the course of each partner's career? Guston liked to think his encounters with writers left some trace on their work. "Clark is becoming less 'Purist,' less 'Reductivist' the more he comes here and Roth, when I see him becomes more 'abstract,' more 'metaphysical'—after an evening with me—Well, friendships *are* based on influencing—so I may turn everything all around,"[54] he declared. However, the affect was not quite so unilateral. That Guston admitted a poet's words into his art, that he was eager to engage in a double billing, disrupted the once monolithic nature of his work, a seismic occurrence for an artist conditioned to the aggrandizement of his individuality.

Debra Bricker Balken

to which you've led it by your mind,
bicycling no-hands
leaving it gasping
there, wondering where you are and how to get back,
although you'll never let
it go
while somewhere everything's dispersed
at five o'clock
for Martinis a group of professional freshnesses meet
and the air's like a shrub—Rose o'Sharon? the others,
it's not
a flickering light for us, but the glare of the dark
too much endlessness
stored up, and in store:
"the exquisite prayer
to be new each day
brings to the artist
only a certain kneeness"
I am assuming that everything is all right and difficult, where hordes of stars
carry the burdens of the gentler animals like ourselves with wit
and austerity beneath a hazardous settlement which we understand
because we made
and secretly admire
because it moves
yes! for always, for it is our way, to pass the tea-house and the ceremony by
and rather fall sobbing to the floor with joy and freezing than to spill
the kid upon the table and then thank the blood
for flowing
as it must throughout the miserable, clear and willful
life we love beneath the blue,
a fleece of pure intention sailing like
a pinto in a barque of slaves
who soon will turn upon their captors
lower anchor, found a city riding there
of poverty and sweetness paralleled
among the races without time,
and one alone will speak of being
born in pain
and he will be the wings of an extraordinary liberty

PLATE 10

39

1. Clark Coolidge, quoted in Debra Bricker Balken, "Combined Aesthetics: Philip Guston & Clark Coolidge," *Art New England*, vol. 11 no. 3 (March 1990), 14.

2. Philip Guston, quoted in Mark Stevens, "A Talk with Philip Guston," *The New Republic*, March 15, 1980, 27.

3. The transformation which took place in Guston's work around 1967–68 is well rehearsed in the writing on the artist and requires no further elaboration here. Cf., for example, Dore Ashton, *Yes, but ... A Critical Study of Philip Guston* (New York: Viking, 1976) and Robert Storr, *Philip Guston* (New York: Abbeville, 1986).

4. Hilton Kramer, "A Mandarin Artist Pretending to be a Stumblebum," *The New York Times*, October 25, 1970, Section B, 22.

5. Clark Coolidge, quoted in "Combined Aesthetics," 14.

6. Philip Guston, letter to Bill Berkson, December 28, 1975, University of Connecticut Library, Storrs, CT.

7. The author was unable to locate the where-abouts of the original drawing for this book.

8. Philip Guston, letter to William Corbett, October 22, 1975.

9. Philip Guston, letter to Bill Berkson, October 4, 1974, University of Connecticut Library, Storrs, CT.

10. O. Henry, "The Gift of the Magi," *Art News Annual*, vol. (1946–47), 69–76. The author is grateful to Bill Berkson for bringing this illustrated essay to her attention.

11. Robert Creeley, "Philip Guston: A Note," *The Black Mountain Review*, no. 6 (Spring 1956), 170–174.

12. Francine du Plessix, "Painters and Poets," *Art in America*, vol. 53, no. 5 (October/November 1965), 24ff.

13. Philip Guston, letter to Bill Berkson, July 15, 1970, University of Connecticut Library, Storrs, CT.

14. Bill Berkson, "The New Gustons," *Art News*, vol. 69, no. 6 (October 1970), 46–47.

15. Clark Coolidge, quoted in *ibid.*, 44.

16. Philip Guston, letter to Bill Berkson, November 6, 1973, University of Connecticut Library, Storrs, CT.

17. Bill Berkson, letter to Philip Guston, October 18, 1973.

18. Correspondence from Guston to Berkson and William Corbett suggests a spate of *Poem-Pictures* were executed in 1975. However, Coolidge seems to recall that these drawings were issued over a period of time that spanned the early 1970s through the mid to latter part of the decade. Cf. Debra Bricker Balken, *Drawings from the Philip Guston and Clark Coolidge Exchange* (Pittsfield, Massachusetts: The Berkshire Museum, 1990).

19. Philip Guston, letter to Bill Berkson, March 23, 1973, University of Connecticut Library, Storrs, CT.

20. Philip Guston, letter to Bill Berkson, January 4, 1972.

21. Philip Guston, letter to William Corbett, October 22, 1975.

22. Clark Coolidge, quoted in "Combined Aesthetics," 14.

23. Philip Guston, letter to Bill Berkson, March 20, 1972, University of Connecticut Library, Storrs, CT.

24. Philip Guston, letter to Dore Ashton, May 17, 1974, University of Connecticut Library, Storrs, CT.

25. Clark Coolidge, quoted in "Combined Aesthetics," 13.

26. *ibid.*

27. Clark Coolidge, letter to Bill Berkson, August 18 1968, University of Connecticut Library, Storrs, CT.

28. For a discussion on the role of publisher in engineering collaborations between artists and writers, cf. Debra Bricker Balken, "Notes on the publisher as auteur," *Art Journal*, vol. 52, no. 4 (December 1993), 70–72.

29. William Corbett, "Philip Guston Drawing Poems," *Notus*, vol. 4, no. 2 (Fall 1989): 3.

30. *ibid.*

31. "Drawings from the Philip Guston and Clark Coolidge Exchange".

32. William Corbett, "What a Miracle Images Are!" *Arts Magazine*, vol. 63, no. 3 (November 1988), 53.

33. Stanley Kunitz, "Remembering Guston," *Next-to-Last Things: New Poems and Essays* (New York: Atlantic Monthly Press, 1985), 73.

34. Philip Guston, letter to Dore Ashton, May 17, 1974, Archives of American Art, Smithsonian Institution.

35. *ibid.*

36. Musa Mayer, Guston's daughter, recalls, "My mother was always the first to see his completed work. When he finished a painting, in the middle of the night, he'd often wake her, too exhilarated to sleep or wait for the morning to share it with her.... Her opinion was crucial to him; he'd watch her face to see if it registered enthusiasm. "What shall we call it?" my father would ask. But when my mother gave him suggestions, she tells me, he would invariably find a title of his own." Cf. *Night Studio: A Memoir of Philip Guston* (New York: Alfred A. Knopf, 1988), 89.

37. Philip Guston, interview with Karl Fortess, April 24, 1966, Archives of American Art, Smithsonian Institution.

38. This list comes from Ashton, *op.cit.*, 80.

39. *op.cit.*, 124.

40. Philip Guston, letter to Dore Ashton, August 25, 1974, Archives of American Art, Smithsonian Institution.

41. Philip Guston, quoted in Stevens, *op.cit.*, 26.

42. "Philip Guston Talking," in *Philip Guston: Paintings, 1969–80*, ex.cat. (London: The Whitechapel Gallery), 54.

43. *ibid.*

44. Philip Guston, letter to Dore Ashton, May 17, 1974, Archives of American Art, Smithsonian Institution.

45. Philip Roth, "Breast Baring," *Vanity Fair*, October 1989, 98.

46. Philip Guston, quoted in John Baur, *Nature in Abstraction* (New York: Whitney Museum of American Art, 1958), 40.

47. Philip Guston and Harold Rosenberg, "Philip Guston's Object," in *Philip Guston: Recent Paintings and Drawings* (New York: The Jewish Museum, 1966), unpaginated.

48. Philip Guston, quoted in "Night Studio," 141.

49. Philip Guston, letter to William Corbett, December 1974.

50. Dore Ashton, "This Is Not What I Mean At All: Why Philip Guston Is Not Postmodern," *Arts Magazine*, vol. 63, no. 3 (November 1988), 71.

51. Jan Butterfield, "Philip Guston—A Very Anxious Fix," *Images and Issues*, vol. 1, no.1 (Summer 1980), 31.

52. Philip Guston, quoted in Brad Gooch, *City Poet: The Life and Times of Frank O'Hara* (New York: Alfred A. Knopf, 1993), 11.

53. From COLLECTED POEMS by Frank O'Hara. copyright © 1958 by Maureen Granville-Smith, Administratrix of the Estate of Frank O'Hara. Reprinted by permission of Alfred A. Knopf Inc.

54. Philip Guston, letter to Dore Ashton September 4, 1974, Archives of American Art, Smithsonian Institution.

ENIGMA
VARIATIONS

PLATE 11

The Ideal Reader

For me, Philip Guston became a hero and a friend almost simultaneously. He was nearing 50, I was in my early twenties. I remember going with Frank O'Hara to his studio one flight up in an old firehouse on West 18th Street and for the first time experiencing that peculiar, separate circumstance: a New York painter's studio packed with elements of a substitute world. A weight in the air differed from the buzz or frantic mess of other painters' lofts. The ambience was other than business as usual. Philip later recalled that I had been strangely silent. I'm sure that was true; I had no answer for being thunderstruck. The next day, annotating my memory of the scene in a journal, I scratched the word "INTEGRITY" in tall spindly letters, as if, for this initiate, the spectral cliché of artistic probity had suddenly broken clear, an old-time value that walked right up, extended a meaty, capable hand, "Greetings."

In Michael Blackwood's film of Guston at work, we see the beautiful gesture Guston makes as he walks slowly back towards his picture in progress to put on more paint: he looks to be swimming in air like a Chinese dancer, and the hand not holding the brush is raised, masking off an area of the composition as he zeroes in. It's still a composition at this point, and on the voice-over commentary he's saying: "Well, everybody has notions. But notions are not reality. Reality is when you feel to take pink paint and you put it down and for some mysterious reason, some magical way, it becomes a hand. Then that's painting The public, the looker, thinks you have a blueprint for it—and there isn't a blueprint...."

Seeing Guston's work around 1960 was a confirmation for me, as much as any poem, that the seemingly arbitrary, often hesitant way of writing I was then pursuing was not mistaken and that even my doubts might generate some worthwhile thing. What he said about his own work was right on target, too: "I just want to nail something so it stays put"; "You work to divest yourself of what you know"; "I want to end with something that will baffle me for some time."

Later he and I could laugh that he became an "Ideal Reader" for the poems—because copying them out with a quill in bold, cleanly spaced lettering and drawing around them, he opened up certain of my poems for me, as to subject. Typically, Philip pondered both the process and the outcome. In a postscript to one of his mid-seventies letters he wrote, "Poems and drawings give each other new powers—energies?" He took it upon himself to "picture" whatever he read that, ever unpredictably, had meaning for him.

Personally, we didn't see very much of each other. Eventually, living in different towns, and then on different coasts, our friendship peaked in exchanges of letters. When we did get together during those late years—once in San Francisco and a few more times in Woodstock—there was always that charge, everything left to say.

Enigma Variations was the realization of a project we had talked about intermittently, the idea of putting together in book form some of my poems with drawings by Philip. In 1974, four years after moving to California, I finally got up the gumption to send Philip a short manuscript with the suggestion that he might put some drawings to the poems, and we could then have a

To Bill   Philip Guston
                 Roma '71

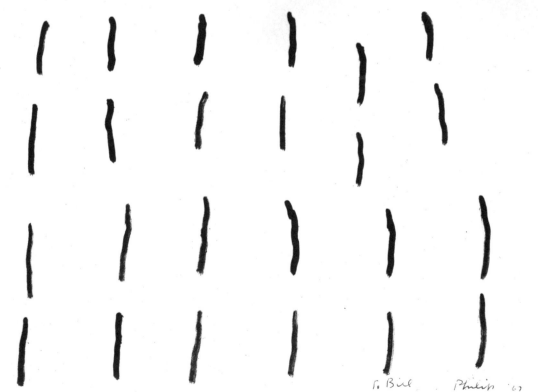

To Bill   Philip '67

PLATES 12, 13

book, "our book." He responded with stunning alacrity: within a month or so, he sent eighteen drawings, each with a note attached telling why that particular drawing went with the designated poem.

The idea was, yes, collaboration, although collaboration a continent apart and by design rather than hands-on. I had already written the poems, and only one of them with Guston especially in mind. Guston, for his part, made some drawings expressly in response to certain poems, but most he selected from work done in more or less the same time frame, 1967–74. Further, as Philip said warily, the drawings should not be seen to "illustrate," but rather to accompany, the poems. ("Illuminate" was an alternate verb we both felt comfortable with.) Thus, the poems and drawings "read" one another across the margins, so to speak, incisively.

There are about a dozen of Guston's paintings and drawings in our home. First, an ink drawing I picked out in late 1962 during my first visit to the Woodstock studio. I had written a somewhat overwrought appreciation in *Kulchur* of his Guggenheim retrospective earlier that year, and Guston liked my account well enough to offer a gift. The drawing is one of those non-stop weaving ones with many loose ends. Near the top is a circle, ambiguous about its relation to gravity—it could be either a balloon or a rock. In the middle, another funny shape, squared-off at one end and narrow like a cardboard box (the kind for long, thin charcoal) and tapering in the other direction like a syringe. Then down below is a fat sort of *schlong* that, but for its size, might have been a tracing of someone's thumb in profile pressed flat. This drawing has all the mystery and canniness in a slow accumulation of image I admired from the start.

Then there is the "primary lesson" of four little paintings on Masonite sent just before my son was born. Reading from left to right across the living room wall: an open blank book; a personal mailbox with a brick on top; a red cup, half in shadow, huge against registers of grey, black, green; and a bulky, tufted easy chair, flat dirty white dotted and edged with black. "Dear Bill, As I was mounting these little oils, I thought how nice they would look hung on your wall as a cluster, joining the small one you have of a canvas on an easel. They look to me like a primary lesson— The Book, The Chair, The Cup, and of course The Mailbox—also as a little present to you & Lynn and baby. Soon, no? Naturally, the book is for baby—not a mark on it—yet—clean. All you will need is a hammer (I mean, to hang them on the wall)."

As fate would have it, it fell to a group of disparate young poets, including myself, to be the core audience for Guston's work during the early seventies, when he had pretty much absented himself from the New York art world, and vice versa. In turn, each of us got the Guston we needed, or deserved—in our lives, for the poems. (It says something about the fitness of his world, I think, that he could feel at home with our diversities.) Guston in person was as changeable, as inclusive, as fierce, as articulate as his paintings. Among friends, the same sweep that manifested terror and absurdity in his art transmuted itself to a social grace—expansive was how he appeared, even when probing introspectively. Philip's charm could take some devilish turns, but his flattery, if that's what it was, registered a will to elevate each instance of artistic friendship to the most plausible Olympian ledge.

Bill Berkson

Bolinas, California, November, 1993

W hat did we want to see? And then, a bit further on, what did we think we would? There were conversations. There was smoking in the chair, with nobody else there. A bright eye, a finger at some recent center, and always back to the work. I doubt we ever *decided* anything. Certainly not a final form for this two-handed book we were always sidling toward. This continuous thinking, or was it worrying?, always so far from the actual working. But the talk, maybe not so separate?

He asked me to draw for him one time. I sketched the chair in front of me in short detached strokes. No, never lift your hand from the paper till the line runs out.

The best clues went into the work and are no longer in my mind.

Started with the specific matter of words and arrived at the utter immateriality of the painted image. Sieved both through the same divide. That neither rest on any surface but move on in the mind. What you see, what your read, is not *this*.

As if children before the buzzing machines coming. I think these were some of the things that entered our conversation:
Eliot's "garlic and sapphires in the mud."
Joyce's labyrinths.
Have you ever been caught between the hovering substances?
The image that locks itself in too quickly so has to be wiped out because it does not go on.
The thin line between image and chaos.
There is no memory print of ecstasy.
Forms that are two: things moving together and things moving away.
The third hand that's at work when it all comes together.
The clear enigma, to be reached.
The drawing stick in that paw's hand.
Images that are surrounded by their history and the rare ones that aren't.
To draw up the Principles of Discontent?
Looking for the one static "Egyptian" form from which all the multitudinous forms come.
To do what nature doesn't do: the single form that keeps vibrating forever.
The times when movement substitutes itself as a form.
What about the masked, and the exposed?
Painting a book in the dark.
Art being the frustration of the desire *not* to make art.
Beckett's disgust and Fellini's hunger.
Melville's wicked book and Kafka's lightless image.
Frankenstein's bangs.
All the blocks that matter.
Maybe a city two guys put up in their spare time.
Trying to decipher the Salami Stone.

"art could be a grimace

you subdue it to a simple door ...

the madmen brothers of nothing said

all begins with images

I join by images"

—Paul Eluard, *To Picasso*

but I could be mistaken. I know that I am not conscious enough while involved, so often deny the memory at its source. And now almost twenty years have passed.

We wanted to make the drawing space and the writing space simultaneous. We believed that it was, anyway. No matter what we particularly did.

CC—2194

... A CAR PART. AND THEN A HUSK. AND NEXT A HEAD. ANDS HOOKED TO CYCLES...

CLARK COOLIDGE

PLATE 14

47

To draw is to make be more than one start.........

CLARK COOLIDGE

PLATE 15

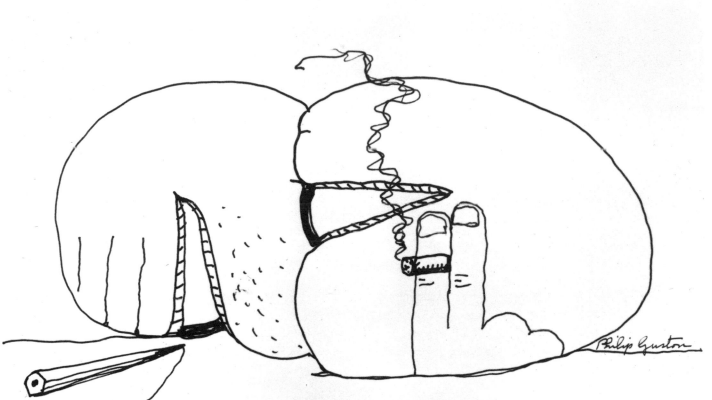

...SMOKING AND DRAWING,
BOTH THOUGHTS OF ANOTHER FINGER.
CIRCLES, BOTH TIME AND LIGHT ENOUGH
FOR ALL STOPS ON ONE LINE...

CLARK COOLIDGE

PLATE 16

TO RELEASE IT NEEDS A GRIP SO STRONG
ONE IS POSSESSED TO COME FREE.

CLARK COOLIDGE

PLATE 17

...I need to
stand away from all I can see.
But all I do is make marks that
begin to resemble things I left
behind me..........

CLARK COOLIDGE

PLATE 18

I have a large dog I taught to lie still.
A thinness that eats room..........
....To lie down for a fire......

CLARK COOLIDGE

PLATE 19

WHOBODY...   ...90.

1.

write on this.
do this.
to this.
an end isn't.
and done.
over this to here.
of down.
and and.
to end it.
this is what.
what that.
do that too.
written and
do to and.
due time.
do tell.

a bore lump.
everything it wills it clad.
shown some closed yet.
amber close.
amid behind in toto.
calendric as salad.
of much past seem means.
cork latch.
fool angle a midge.
coily doubt.
eye ruled sheets.
stem doubly.
lumpy as a star raising.
floor ouncing.
as can treats.
the mum.
the sighed it.
ub iwerks.

Clark Coolidge . . . . . .

Philip Guston '73

PLATE 20

53

.....I KICKED INTO
PRECISE
SPACE
WITHOUT TOUCHING.

I SPENT CHEESE
AS A SENTENCE. **RAIN**
TO
STOP
BREATHING.

BODY CLAW ENOUGH
TO SMILE A CRACK. LEAVE
THESE
THINGS

LIE ENOUGH TO GET BUILDING...

CLARK COOLIDGE

PLATE 21

LINES, DROPS.

To Draw AS ROCKS SLIP THEIR LOCKS MEET HUNKS.

TO DRAW AS ROCKS SLIP THEIR LOCKS

LIGHT UNDER A PYRAMID. AND DREAM SHARPENING

the skull out of paper.

CLARK COOLIDGE

PLATE 22

...I am the first to have seen where I live. Whether I am or not, in turn. Light on the chair. Book sat in the wall......

CLARK COOLIDGE

PLATE 23

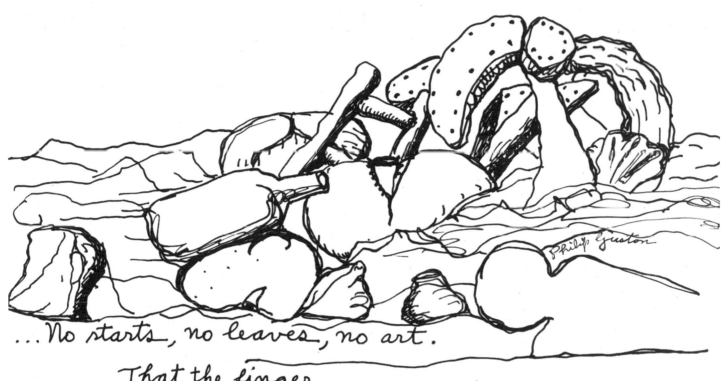

...No starts, no leaves, no art.

That the finger
points that the foot kicks. But
the head is a clock in a pile of
stuff that clocks heads.

Art is no longer
having to make a move ...

CLARK COOLIDGE

PLATE 24

PLATE 25

.....Seeing creatures in my own
furrows,
feeling the curling mass of earth
won't release me.

CLARK COOLIDGE

On Philip Guston

Philip Guston was a hero who became a friend. We mostly saw each other during the years he came to Boston for a few days each month to teach at Boston University. Mornings after we spent the night talking the candle down, I always felt the desire to write, to get down to *it*. Such was the power of Philip's talk, the like of which I will be fortunate to encounter again. Philip knew in his bones the dignity and worth of art-making. While he doubted every aspect of this endeavor, these were the doubts of a believer. He inspired me to explore the most private and feared territory of my imagination. Part of who I am today began to take shape on those nights in our conversations.

The poem-drawings (we had no word for them) Philip made of my work did not draw on the time we spent together, at least not directly. Of course, I knew the drawings he had done of his wife Musa's poems and those of our mutual friend Clark Coolidge, but I could only hope that Philip might favor my work with such attention. When he agreed to do the cover for *Columbus Square Journal*, I sent him the manuscript then titled "Columbus Day A Year." My ear cringed at that title's dying fall, but no alternative came to me. It was with great delight that I saw the title Philip gave the book. He combined the street I live on with the book's form. Perfect!

I was even more delighted when Philip and Musa came for dinner in the fall of 1976. He had under his arm a large homemade cardboard portfolio from which he took thirteen drawings of poems of mine, all but two from the journal. Except for "The Richard Nixon Story," a subject we never tired of discussing, I have no idea what attracted Philip to the poems he drew, and to my surprise I never asked. Indeed, I could only thank him that night and marvel at what he had done and the generosity of his gift.

What I see in these drawings today is Philip's hand expressing his reader's imagination. But that, accurate as it is, places the hand too far from the mind. I see here, as in so much of Philip's late work, the hand and mind as one. What he imagined, he drew. A direct connection. In these drawings Philip is, I think, "reading" my poems, and what we see is the associations my poems called up for him. They could be x-rays of his imagination, and I know that I had never before "seen" anyone read my poems.

I also see something else that has only coincidentally to do with my work. Philip made these drawings in the summer when he was on one of his runs and painting up a storm of who knows how many paintings. So inspired (it is too mild a word) was he that he transformed everything into his images. He could not walk the twenty-five feet from his kitchen door to his studio without his brain teeming and his hand twitching for one of his bamboo drawing pens. I see here the fever that was on him through those years and feel its surge as I follow the surge of his lines.

William Corbett

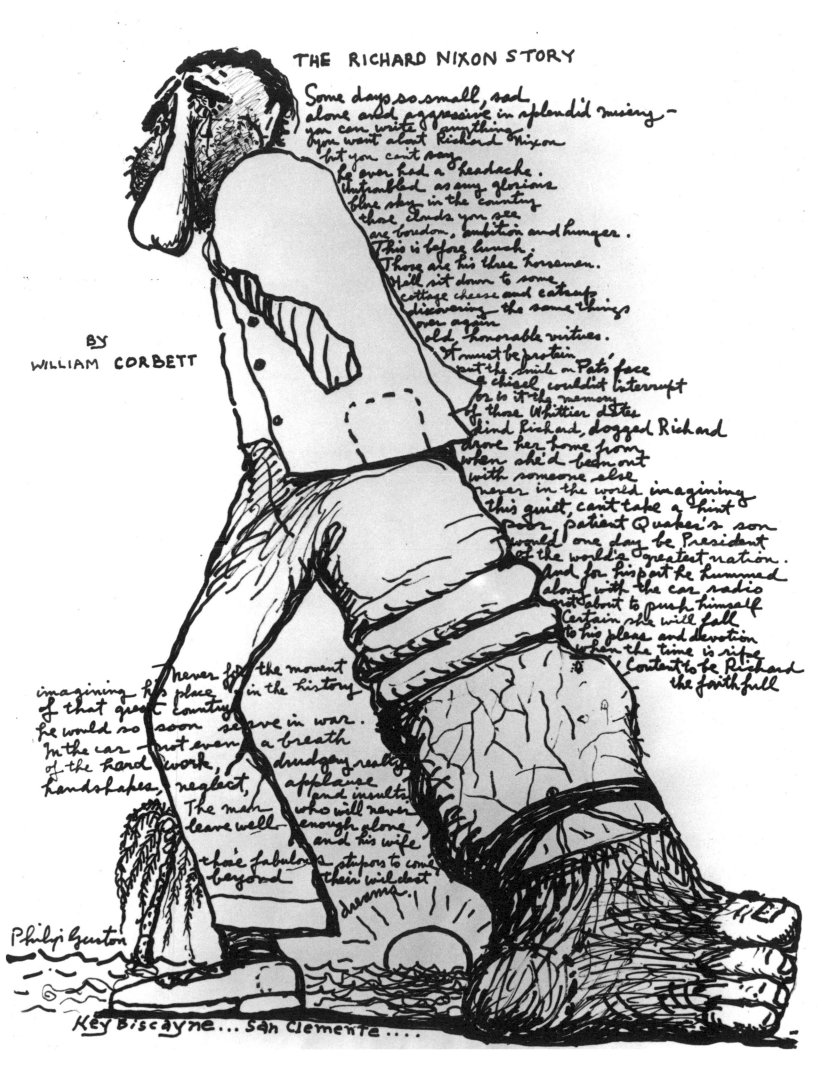

THE RICHARD NIXON STORY

BY
WILLIAM CORBETT

Some days so small, sad,
alone and aggressive in splendid misery —
you can write anything
you want about Richard Nixon
but you can't say
he ever had a headache.
Untroubled as any glorious
blue sky in the country
those clouds you see
are boredom, ambition and hunger.
This is before lunch.
Those are his three horsemen.
He'll sit down to some
cottage cheese and catsup
discovering the same things
over again
old, honorable virtues.
It must be protein
put the smile on Pat's face
a chisel couldn't interrupt
or is it the memory
of those Whittier dates
blind Richard, dogged Richard
drove her home from
when she'd been out
with someone else
never in the world imagining
this quiet, can't take a hint
poor patient Quaker's son
would one day be President
of the world's greatest nation.
And for his part he hummed
along with the car radio
not about to push himself
Certain she will fall
to his place and devotion
when the time is ripe
Content to be Richard
the faithfull

never for the moment
imagining his place   in the history
of that great country
he would so soon   serve in war.
In the car — not even   a breath
of the hard work,   drudgery really,
handshakes, neglect,   applause
and insults
The man   who will never
leave well   enough alone
and his wife
those fabulous stupors to come
beyond   their wildest
dreams.

Philip Guston

Key Biscayne ... San Clemente ....

PLATE 26

Easter......

WILLIAM CORBETT

Waking Easter morning,
soft gray morning grey like
the settling of city dust
on windowsills and walls
waking on a couch
under the red slipcover
remembering New York
upper West Side twelve years ago
friends not seen since when?
Wondering about the lives
of friends in the next room
theorizing about their life
pleasant to do half asleep
wondering, as always, if they love me
if I love them and what
our lives together hold for us.

Philip Guston

PLATE 27

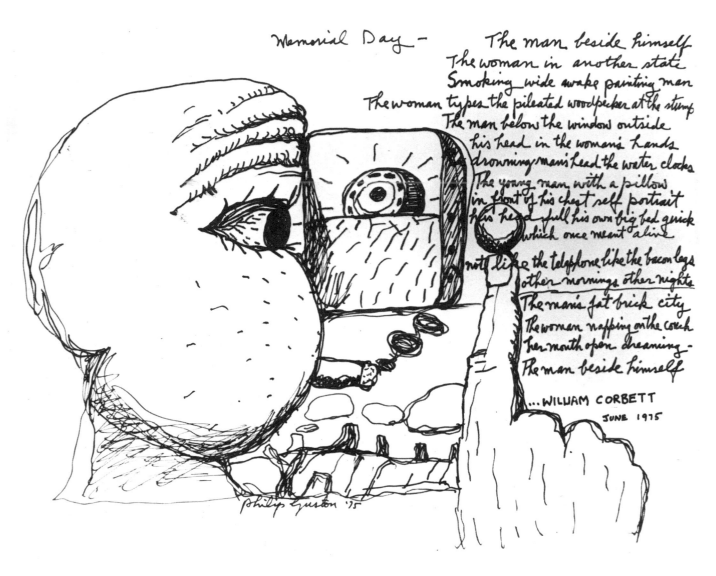

Memorial Day —

The man beside himself
The woman in another state
Smoking wide awake painting man
The woman types the pileated woodpecker at the stump
The man below the window outside
his head in the woman's hands
drowning man's head the water clocks
The young man with a pillow
in front of his chest self portrait
his head full his own big bed quick
which once meant alive
not like the telephone like the bacon legs
other mornings other nights
The man's fat brick city
The woman napping on the couch
her mouth open dreaming —
The man beside himself

...WILLIAM CORBETT
JUNE 1975

PLATE 28

63

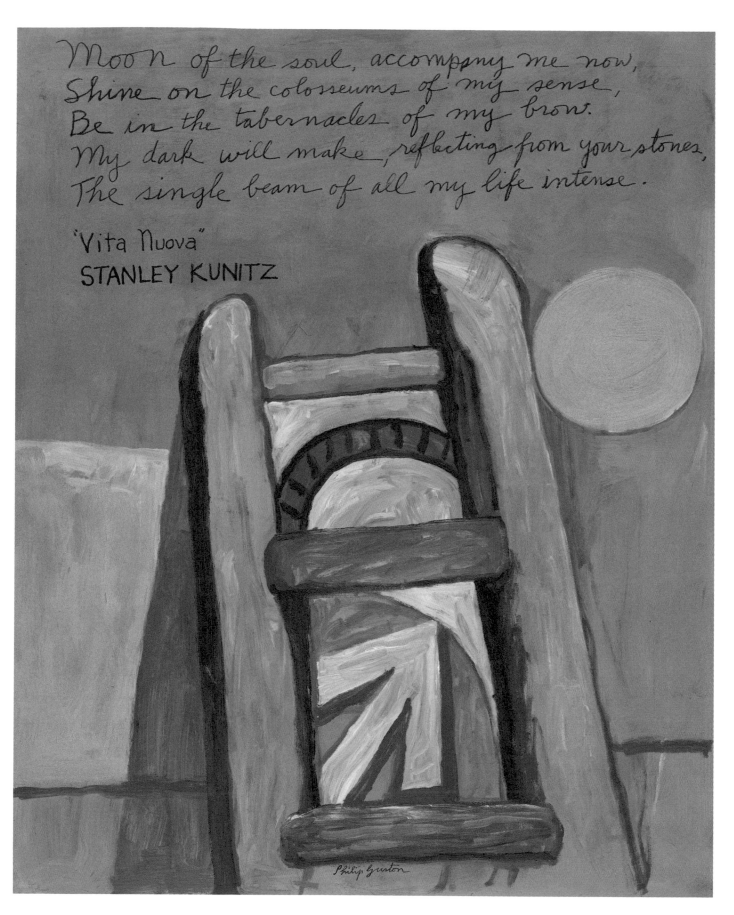

Moon of the soul, accompany me now,
Shine on the colosseums of my sense,
Be in the tabernacles of my brow.
My dark will make, reflecting from your stones,
The single beam of all my life intense.

'Vita Nuova"
STANLEY KUNITZ

Philip Guston

PLATE 29

Remembering Guston

Of all the artists I have been close to through the years, Philip Guston was unquestionably the most daemonic. This daemon in him had an enormous appetite—for life and art and food and drink and friendship and, I mustn't forget, talk—not gossip or frivolous banter, but high talk through the night on the grand themes that agitate a serious mind, excited talk, with little pockets of moisture bubbling at the corners of his mouth. Others who drifted in and out of the room eventually collapsed or disappeared; but at dawn Philip was still in top form, replenishing his vehemence with a last or next-to-last nightcap, as we raided the refrigerator and brewed a fresh pot of coffee. That is my image of Philip from the fifties and sixties, before he turned his back on the New York art world and settled permanently with Musa in Woodstock, a move that somehow signaled for me the end of an era, the breaking-up of a world of exhilarating companionships. Things were never quite the same after that.

Volcanic is another word I think of in connection with Philip. He did not so much occupy his physical frame as seethe within it. His rage was always perilously close to the surface, ready for instantaneous eruption, attended by a darkening of his whole countenance and a creasing of his brow. On such occasions you could almost watch the horns growing out of his temples. He did not suffer fools gladly, or at all. About his work he was superlatively touchy. Once a woman, a stranger, gave him a lift from a party. As they were driving along, she made polite conversation by telling him that she preferred his older paintings to his new. "Stop the car!" Philip shouted and jumped out on the highway.

In 1976, when I was Consultant in Poetry to the Library of Congress, the Smithsonian Institution commissioned him, in collaboration with me, to design a poster celebrating the marriage of poetry and painting. The poster that he executed, in his late brutal style, incorporating some of my lines, was an extraordinary work, so powerful in fact that it succeeded in frightening the people at the Smithsonian. As part of our contract, Philip and I agreed to conduct a public dialogue in Washington, but the event was cancelled on the eve. "Bastards!" cried Philip. "They think they can treat us like a pair of old farts!" And then, as if to compensate for our failed expectations, he made a beautiful gesture, presenting me with the original painting—oil on paper—together with a set of magnificent drawings based on other poems of mine that he favored. These are treasures.

How much Philip loved poetry! One of my most vivid recollections is of an evening when I read the poems of Hopkins aloud to him at his request, for he had never heard them spoken. There were a few other friends in the room, but what I concentrated on was his face, aglow, as I had scarcely seen it before, except when he talked of Piero della Francesca, who stood in his eyes for the incorruptible glory of art.

My heart is hiding

Stirred for a bird,—the achieve of, the mastery of the thing!

Brute beauty and valour and act, oh, air, pride, plume here

   Buckle! AND the fire that breaks from thee then, a billion

   Times told lovelier, more dangerous, O my chevalier!

   No wonder of it: shéer plód makes plough down sillion

Shine, and blue-bleak embers, ah my dear,

   Fall, gall themselves, and gash gold-vermilion.

Stanley Kunitz

the folded message in his hands
is •stiff with dirt and wine-stains,

older than the
Dead Sea Scrolls.

Daughter, read:

What do I want of my life?
More! More!

STANLEY KUNITZ

from "Journal for My Daughter"

PLATE 30

Selected Bibliography

ARTIST/WRITER COLLABORATIONS

Balken, Debra Bricker. "In the Collaborative Tradition," *Guggenheim Magazine*, vol. 1, no. 3 (Summer 1993), 30–31.

Balken, ed. "Interactions between artists and writers," *Art Journal*, vol. 52, no. 4 (Winter 1993).

Berkson, Bill. "It's raining/and I'm thinking …" *Poem-paintings by Frank O'Hara and Norman Bluhm*. exh. cat. New York: Loeb Student Center, New York University, 1967.

Burroughs, William and Gysin, Brion. *The Third Mind*. New York: The Viking Press, 1978.

Diggory, Terence. *Grace Hartigan and the Poets: Paintings and Prints*. exh. cat. Saratoga Springs, New York: Schick Gallery, Skidmore Gallery, 1993.

Hines, Thomas Jensen. *Collaborative Form: Studies in the Relations of the Arts*. Kent, Ohio: Kent State University Press, 1991.

Hubert, Renée Riese. *Surrealism and the Book*. Berkeley, California: University of California Press, 1988.

Koestenbaum, Wayne. *Double Talk: The Erotics of Male Literary Collaboration*. New York: Routledge, 1989.

Koch, Kenneth, "A Note of this Issue," *Locus Solus*, no. 2 (1961), 193–197.

Kunitz, Stanley. "Editorial: The Sister Arts," *Art in America*, vol. 53, no. 5 (October/November 1965), 23.

Lanchner, Carolyn. *Sophie Taeuber-Arp*. exh. cat. New York: The Museum of Modern Art, 1981.

Nathan, Jean. "How a Painting Inspired a Novella & Other Stories," *Art News*, vol. 92, no. 5 (September 1993), 160–163.

Perloff, Marjorie. *Frank O'Hara, Poet Among Painters*. New York: George Braziller, 1977.

Plessix, Francine du. "Painters and Poets," *Art in America*, vol. 53, no. 5 (October/November 1965), 24ff.

Rivers, Larry. "Life Among the Stones," *Location*, vol. 1, no.1 (Spring 1963), 90–96.

Rogoff, Irgit, "Production Lines," in *Team Spirit*. exh. cat. New York: Independent Curators Incorporated, 1991.

Shapiro, David. "Art as Collaboration, Toward a Theory of Pluralist Aesthetics 1950–1980," in *Artistic Collaboration in the Twentieth Century*, ed. Cynthia Jaffee Macabe. exh. cat. Washington, D.C.: Smithsonian Institution Press and the Hirshhorn Museum and Sculpture Garden, 1984.

Shapiro. *Poets and Painters*. exh. cat. Denver: Denver Art Museum, 1980.

Steiner, Wendy. *Pictures of Romance: Form against Context in Painting and Literature*. Chicago: University of Chicago Press, 1988.

Yau, John. "Collectif Generation," *Collectif Generation, Livres d'Artistes*. London: Victoria and Albert Museum, 1990.

GUSTON'S EXCHANGES WITH WRITERS

Ashton, Dore. *Yes, but … A Critical Study of Philip Guston*. New York: The Viking Press, 1976.

Balken, Debra Bricker. "Afterword to 16 Poems For Philip Guston," *TO*, no. 4 (Spring 1994), 53–54.

Balken. "Combined Aesthetics: Philip Guston & Clark Coolidge," *Art New England*, vol. 11, no. 3 (March 1990), 13–14.

Balken *Drawings from the Philip Guston and Clark Coolidge Exchange*. exh. cat. Pittsfield, Massachusetts: The Berkshire Museum, 1990.

Berkson, Bill. "The New Gustons," *Art News*, vol. 69, no. 6 (October 1970), 44–47, 85.

Corbett, William. "Philip Guston/Clark Coolidge." *Arts Magazine*, vol. 65, no.10 (Summer 1991), 67.

Corbett. "What a Miracle Images Are!" *Arts Magazine*, vol. 63, no. 3 (November 1988), 51–54.

Corbett. "Philip Guston Drawing Poems," *Notus*, vol. 4, no. 2 (Fall 1989), 3.

Corbett. *Philip Guston's Late Works: A Memoir*. Cambridge, Massachusetts: Zoland Press, 1994.

Creeley, Robert. "Philip Guston: A Note," *The Black Mountain Review*, no. 6 (Spring 1956), 170–174.

Roth, Philip. "Breast Baring," *Vanity Fair*, October, 1989, 94–99.

Rubinstein, Meyer Raphael. "Philip Guston and Clark Coolidge at Galerie Lelong," *Art in America*, vol. 79, no. 7 (July 1991), 123.

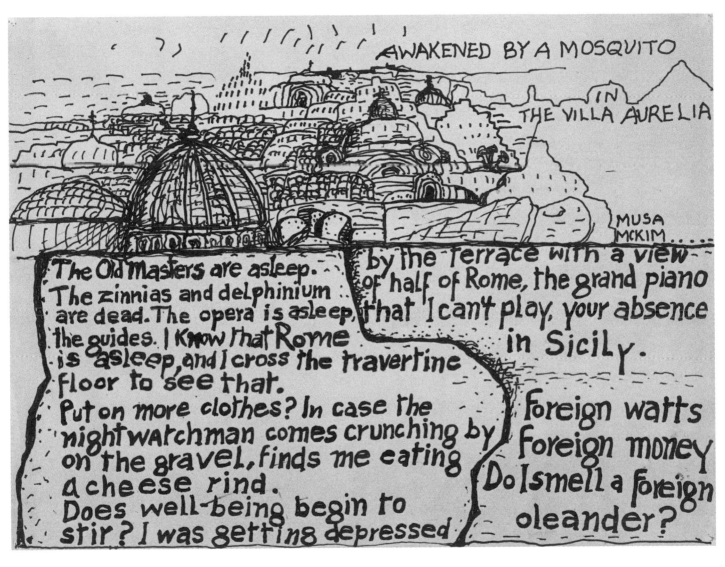

The Old Masters are asleep.
The zinnias and delphinium
are dead. The opera is asleep,
the guides. I know that Rome
is asleep, and I cross the travertine
floor to see that.
Put on more clothes? In case the
nightwatchman comes crunching by
on the gravel, finds me eating
a cheese rind.
Does well-being begin to
stir? I was getting depressed
by the terrace with a view
of half of Rome, the grand piano
that I can't play, your absence
in Sicily.

foreign watts
foreign money
Do I smell a foreign
oleander?

AWAKENED BY A MOSQUITO
IN THE VILLA AURELIA

MUSA McKIM . . . .

PLATE 31

YOU

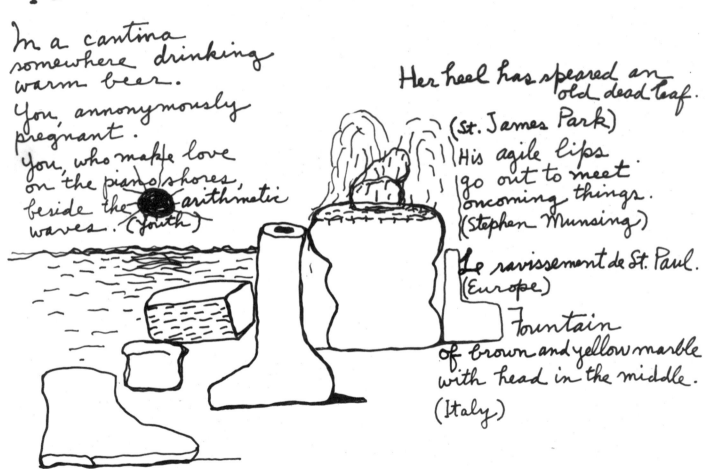

In a cantina
somewhere drinking
warm beer.
You, annonymously
pregnant.
You, who make love
on the piano/shores,
beside the ███ arithmetic
waves. (South.)

Her heel has speared an
old dead leaf.
(St. James Park)
His agile lips
go out to meet
oncoming things.
(Stephen Munsing.)

Le ravissement de St. Paul.
(Europe.)

Fountain
of brown and yellow marble
with head in the middle.
(Italy.)

PLATE 32

I thought I would never
write anything down again.

Then I put on my cold wristwatch.

MUSA McKIM

PLATE 33

UNHAPPY DRUGSTORE

THE TEMPERATURE IS FRIGID. THE COUNTER COMES UP TO THE MIDDLE OF THE WAITRESS' THIGH. THE SEATS ARE CRUELLY CLOSE TOGETHER.

THE MAN ON MY LEFT HAS A SMALL MAGAZINE OPEN TO AN ARTICLE ENTITLED "YOUR DENTURES".

TWO WOMEN SPEAK OF SOMEONE THEY KNOW WHO DROPPED DEAD IN A
PEW
IN
CHURCH.

MUSA MᶜKIM

PLATE 34

A BLACK NO

I GOT A BLACK NO, TWO REGULAR NOS, AND A LIGHT NO.

YOU HAVE A REGULAR NO WORKING TOO, EH?

GIVE ME A REGULAR NO, SUGAR ON THE SIDE.

PLATE 35

SUMMER 1953

Dead lacey insects.
Seams stitched with orange
Thread. The red button
Found. Goodnight, sweetly,
And thank you for the riddle.

musa.

PLATE 36

Checklist

BILL BERKSON AND PHILIP GUSTON

Air, 1971
ink on paper
18 x 24 in.
Collection of Bill Berkson

Belgian Reflexes, 1973–74
ink on paper
13 x 16 ½ in.
Collection of Philip Anglim

Cover drawing for *Big Sky 4*, 1973
ink on paper
15 x 21 in.
Collection of Bill Berkson

Camera Ready, Like a Dream, c. 1968
ink on paper
9 ⅞ x 14 ¾ in.
Collection of Bill Berkson

Canto, 1973
ink on paper
17 x 14 in.
Courtesy Gallery Paule Anglim

Daisies, 1973–74
ink on paper
16 ½ x 12 ½ in.
Courtesy Gallery Paule Anglim

Election Day Fog, 1973–74
ink on paper
14 x 12 ¾ in.
Collection of Paul Sack

Untitled cover drawing for *Enigma Variations*
ink on paper
17 x 15 in.
Collection of Bill Berkson

Untitled drawing for *Enigma Variations*
ink on paper
18 x 17 in.
Collection of Bill Berkson

For Robert Smithson, 1973–74
ink on paper
18 ¾ x 15 in.
Courtesy Gallery Paule Anglim

Untitled drawing for *Like Angels*
ink on paper
12 ¾ x 16 ½ in.
Collection of Bill Berkson

Matter, 1969
charcoal on paper
16 x 19 in.
Collection of Bill Berkson

Negative, 1973
ink on paper
24 x 19 in.
Collection of Bill Berkson

Thoughts, 1974
ink on paper
17 ¾ x 24 in.
Collection of Larry Silva

Untitled, 1961
ink on paper
18 x 23 ¾ in.
Collection of Bill Berkson

Untitled (a/no ...), c. 1973–74
ink on paper
10 x 16 ¾ in.
Courtesy Gallery Paule Anglim

Water, 1967
ink on paper
18 x 24 in.
Collection of Bill Berkson

CLARK COOLIDGE AND PHILIP GUSTON

...The Act of Painting
ink on paper
16 x 18 ¾ in.
Collection of Clark Coolidge

The Act of Painting
ink on paper
18 ¾ x 24 in.
Collection of Clark Coolidge

..A Book Like a Brick Loaf
ink on paper
19 x 24 in.
Collection of Clark Coolidge

...Borderlands
ink on paper
19 x 24 in.
Collection of Clark Coolidge

...A Car Part
ink on paper
18 x 24 in.
Collection of Clark Coolidge

Comes Out That It
ink on paper
19 x 24 in.
Collection of Clark Coolidge

The Country Autumns
ink on paper
19 x 24 in.
Collection of Clark Coolidge

The Drawing, 1975
ink on paper
19 x 25 in.
Collection of Clark Coolidge

Every is Stuff is Thing
ink on paper
19 x 24 in.
Collection of Clark Coolidge

Face an Inch from the Earth
ink on paper
19 x 24 in.
Collection of Clark Coolidge

.A Hand Grips Itself
ink on paper
19 x 24 in.
Collection of Clark Coolidge

..The Heart of Weight
ink on paper'
17 x 14 in.
Collection of Clark Coolidge

…I am the First to Have Seen Where I Live
ink on paper
19 x 24 in.
Collection of Clark Coolidge

I Have a Large Dog I Taught to Lie Still
ink on paper
19 x 24 in.
Collection of Clark Coolidge

…..I Kicked Into Precise Space Without Touching
ink on paper
19 x 24 in.
Collection of Clark Coolidge

I Met Myself In A Dream
ink on paper
19 x 24 in.
Collection of Clark Coolidge

…I Need to
ink on paper
19 x 24 in.
Collection of Clark Coolidge

…I Went Down to Stick in the Hole
ink on paper
19 x 24 in.
Collection of Clark Coolidge

…In the Things We See There is So Much Time We Do Not Feel
ink on paper
19 x 25 ³⁄₁₆ in.
Collection of Clark Coolidge

…Landings of Grit State
ink on paper
19 x 24 in.
Collection of Clark Coolidge

Let It All Together, Apart
ink on paper
19 x 17 in.
Collection of Clark Coolidge

Lines, Drops
ink on paper
19 x 24 in.
Collection of Clark Coolidge

…The Need to Pound Apples into a Door
ink on paper
18 x 23 ¾ in.
Collection of Clark Coolidge

…Next To The Painting A Painting
ink on paper
18 ¼ x 23 in.
Collection of Clark Coolidge

No Grip Ever
ink on paper
19 x 24 in.
Collection of Clark Coolidge

…No Starts, No Leaves, No Art
ink on paper
19 x 24 in.
Collection of Clark Coolidge

…..One Must Become, 1975
ink on paper
19 x 25 in.
Collection of Clark Coolidge

The "Oracle", The Cave, The Desert, 1975
ink on paper
19 x 25 1/4 in.
Collection of Clark Coolidge

..The Painter Can't Sleep for Sight Won't Move
ink on paper
19 x 24 in.
Collection of Clark Coolidge

……The Rest is Space
ink on paper
19 x 24 in.
Collection of Clark Coolidge

…..Seeing Creatures in My Own Furrows
ink on paper
19 x 24 in.
Collection of Clark Coolidge

Signs Put Up On A Boundless Space
ink on paper
19 x 25 in.
Collection of Clark Coolidge

…Smoking and Drawing
ink on paper
19 x 24 in.
Collection of Clark Coolidge

…..The Space Between Things
ink on paper
19 x 25 in.
Collection of Clark Coolidge

... Borderlands. A thumb
raises up to spot clear and chalk
white. That the lines are shades are
drawn.

CLARK COOLIDGE

PLATE 37

…Square Tight
ink on paper
19 x 24 in.
Collection of Clark Coolidge

…The Stage is Already So Full With Things
ink on paper
19¼ x 24 in.
Collection of Clark Coolidge

Stand Down
ink on paper
19 x 24 in.
Collection of Clark Coolidge

…A Thing Made by Nothing or Nobody?
ink and graphite on paper
14 x 16¼ in.
Collection of Clark Coolidge

To Draw is to Make Be More Than One Start
ink on paper
19 x 24 in.
Collection of Clark Coolidge

To Release It Needs A Grip So Strong
ink on paper
19 x 24 in.
Collection of Clark Coolidge

1. Whobody… …90
ink on paper
23½ x 19 in.
Collection of Clark Coolidge

A Window On To The Green Bottles
ink on paper
19 x 23¾ in.
Collection of Clark Coolidge

…"The Word Cellar With a Dirt Floor"
ink on paper
19 x 24 in.
Collection of Clark Coolidge

660/224 "The Door," 1973
oil on paper
30 x 40 in.
Collection of Clark Coolidge

WILLIAM CORBETT AND PHILIP GUSTON

9 April, Bored Magic Death, c. 1975
ink on paper
19 x 23⅞ in.
Collection of William Corbett

11 April, Lump Heart
ink on paper
19 x 25⅛ in.
Collection of Jay Boggis

12 April, Walker Evans Dead, c. 1975
ink on paper
19 x 24 in.
Collection of Michael Palmer

Columbus Square Journal
ink on paper
17 x 14 in.
Collection of William Corbett

Easter……, c. 1975
ink on paper
19 x 25⅛ in.
Collection of William Corbett

Memorial Day, 1975
ink on paper
19 x 25 in.
Collection of Ben E. and Judith C. Watkins

The Richard Nixon Story
ink on paper
23¾ x 19 in.
Collection of William Corbett

STANLEY KUNITZ AND PHILIP GUSTON

An Old Cracked Tune, 1976
ink on paper
19 x 24 in.
Collection of Stanley Kunitz

Journal for My Daughter, 1976
ink on paper
19 x 24⅛ in.
Collection of Stanley Kunitz

King of the River, 1976
ink on paper
19 x 24 in.
Collection of Stanley Kunitz

Poster, 1976
red ink and india ink on offset lithograph
25 x 21½ in.
Private Collection, New York

The Testing Tree, 1976
ink on paper
19 x 14 in.
Collection of Stanley Kunitz

Untitled (from "Vita Nuova"), 1976
acrylic on paper
36 x 30 in.
Collection of Stanley Kunitz

Untitled (from "Vita Nuova"), 1976
acrylic on paper
37 x 30 in.
Collection of Stanley Kunitz

In a murderous time

the heart breaks and breaks
and lives by breaking.
It is necessary to go
through dark and deeper dark
and not to turn.
"The Testing-Tree". Stanley Kunitz

PLATE 38

Philip Guston '70

PLATE 39

MUSA McKIM AND PHILIP GUSTON

A Black No
ink on paper
18 x 24 in.
Courtesy Estate of Musa Guston

Alone with the Moon
ink on paper
19½ x 15¼ in.
Courtesy Estate of Musa Guston

Awakened by a Mosquito in the Villa Aurelia
ink on paper
19 x 25¼ in.
Courtesy Estate of Musa Guston

Brooklyns
ink on paper
19⅝ x 14⅛
Courtesy Estate of Musa Guston

Exciting
ink on paper
19 x 24 in.
Courtesy Estate of Musa Guston

French-English, English-French
ink on paper
19 x 24 in.
Courtesy Estate of Musa Guston

Here We Are, There Gabriella Is
ink on paper
19 x 24 in.
Courtesy Estate of Musa Guston

I Thought I would never write anything down again
ink on paper
19 x 24 in.
Courtesy Estate of Musa Guston

The Leaves Have Turned
ink on paper
19 x 25⅛ in.
Courtesy Estate of Musa Guston

The News From Here
ink on paper
19 x 24 in.
Courtesy Estate of Musa Guston

Oh, Oh
ink on paper
19 x 25⅛ in.
Courtesy Estate of Musa Guston

On Your Birthday
ink on paper
19 x 24 in.
Courtesy Estate of Musa Guston

the Season of the Year
ink on paper
23⅝ x 18⅞ in.
Courtesy Estate of Musa Guston

Summer 1953
ink on paper
25 x 19¾ in.
Courtesy Estate of Musa Guston

The Train
ink on paper
18½ x 23½ in.
Courtesy Estate of Musa Guston

Unhappy Drugstore
ink on paper
19 x 24 in.
Courtesy Estate of Musa Guston

What A Day
ink on paper
19 x 24 in.
Courtesy Estate of Musa Guston

Whoever gets there first
ink on paper
19 x 24 in.
Courtesy Estate of Musa Guston

You
ink on paper
19 x 24 in.
Courtesy Estate of Musa Guston

ALICE NOTLEY AND PHILIP GUSTON

Hand and Cigar, 1970
ink on paper
17 x 14 in.
Collection of Edward F. Miller

FRANK O'HARA AND PHILIP GUSTON

Ode to Michael Goldberg ('s Birth and Other Births)
(February 1–3, 1958) from *In Memory of My Feelings*, 1967
six offset prints within book
each sheet 12 x 18 in.
Collection of William Corbett

ANNE WALDMAN AND PHILIP GUSTON

The World, 1974
ink on paper
28 x 16⅞ in.
Collection of Lisa and Stuart Ginsberg

List of Plates

1. Stanley Kunitz and Philip Guston
   Untitled (from "Vita Nuova"), 1976

2. Clark Coolidge and Philip Guston
   The Act of Painting

3. Ann Waldman and Philip Guston
   The World, 1974

4. Musa McKim and Philip Guston
   Alone with the Moon

5. Philip Guston
   Allegory, 1975, oil on canvas, The St. Louis
   Art Museum, Purchase: The Shoenberg
   Foundation, Inc.; Mr. and Mrs. Robert
   Shoenberg, by exchange. (not in
   exhibition)

6. Clark Coolidge and Philip Guston
   .....The Space Between Things

7. Bill Berkson and Philip Guston
   Untitled drawing for *Enigma Variations*

8. Bill Berkson and Philip Guston
   Negative, 1973

9. William Corbett and Philip Guston
   Columbus Square Journal

10. Frank O'Hara and Philip Guston
    *Ode to Michael Goldberg ('s Birth and Other
    Births)* (February 1–3, 1958), pl. 18–6 from
    In Memory of My Feelings, Copyright © 1958
    by Maureen Granville-Smith, Administrix of
    the Estate of Frank O'Hara. Reprinted by
    permission of Alfred A. Knopf Inc.

11. Bill Berkson and Philip Guston
    Untitled cover drawing for *Enigma
    Variations*

12. Bill Berkson and Philip Guston
    Air, 1971

13. Bill Berkson and Philip Guston
    Water, 1967

14. Clark Coolidge and Philip Guston
    ...A Car Part

15. Clark Coolidge and Philip Guston
    To Draw is to Make Be More Than One Start

16. Clark Coolidge and Philip Guston
    ...Smoking and Drawing

17. Clark Coolidge and Philip Guston
    To Release It Needs A Grip So Strong

18. Clark Coolidge and Philip Guston
    ...I Need to

19. Clark Coolidge and Philip Guston
    I Have a Large Dog I Taught to Lie Still

20. Clark Coolidge and Philip Guston
    1. Whobody... ...90

21. Clark Coolidge and Philip Guston
    *.....I Kicked Into Precise Space Without
    Touching*

22. Clark Coolidge and Philip Guston
    Lines, Drops

23. Clark Coolidge and Philip Guston
    ...I am the First to Have Seen Where I Live

24. Clark Coolidge and Philip Guston
    ...No Starts, No Leaves, No Art

25. Clark Coolidge and Philip Guston
    .....Seeing Creatures in My Own Furrows

26. William Corbett and Philip Guston
    The Richard Nixon Story

27. William Corbett and Philip Guston
    Easter....., c. 1975

28. William Corbett and Philip Guston
    Memorial Day, 1975

29. Stanley Kunitz and Philip Guston
    Untitled (from "Vita Nuova"), 1976

30. Stanley Kunitz and Philip Guston
    Journal for My Daughter, 1976

31. Musa McKim and Philip Guston
    Awakened by a Mosquito in the Villa Aurelia

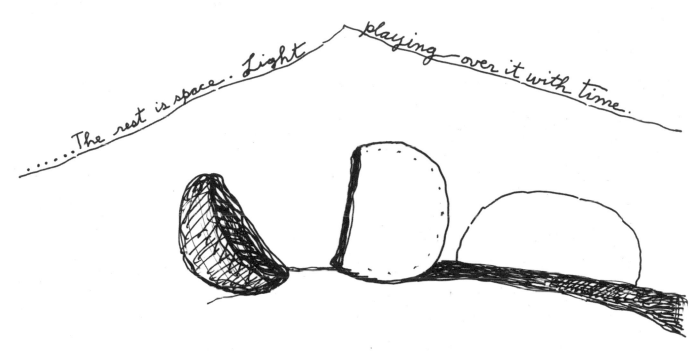

......The rest is space. Light playing over it with time.

or all the things that will be made in the world have been made not otherwise....

CLARK COOLIDGE

Philip Guston

PLATE 40

The rest is space. Light
playing over it with time.....
c.c.

For Susan & Clark. Philip

PLATE 41